CLASSICAL
AUDITION
SPEECHES
for Women

In memory of
Thomas Dogget

'Who it is said took lodgings in Wapping'
in order to perfect his 'Sailor' part in
Love for Love
(performed in 1695)

CLASSICAL AUDITION SPEECHES
for Women

Jean Marlow

A&C Black · London
Heinemann · New Hampshire

First published 1996 by
A & C Black (Publishers) Limited
35 Bedford Row, London WC1R 4JH

ISBN 0–7136–4249–1

© 1996 Jean Marlow

Published simultaneously in the USA by Heinemann
A Division of Reed Publishing (USA) Inc.
361 Hanover Street, Portsmouth, NH 03801–3912
Offices and Agents throughout the world

Distributed in Canada by Reed Books Canada
75 Clegg Road, Markham, Ontario L6G 1A1

ISBN 0-435-07025-8

CIP catalogue records for this book are available
from the British Library and the Library of Congress.

Typeset in $9\frac{1}{2}$ on 12 pt Palatino by
Florencetype Limited, Stoodleigh, Devon

Printed in Great Britain by Redwood Books, Trowbridge, Wilts

Jean Marlow

Jean Marlow, L.G.S.M., a qualified speech and drama teacher (Guildhall School of Music and Drama), is also an actress with many years' experience in theatre, films and television.

From her early days when she worked with a group of actors, writers and directors at the Royal Court Theatre and came under the influence of George Devine, she has played roles as diverse as 'Mrs Ebury' in Tom Stoppard's *Dirty Linen* in the West End, 'Elizabeth Sawyer' in *The Witch of Edmonton*, 'Dol Common' in *Playhouse Creatures* and 'Mrs Jiniwin' in the Walt Disney classic miniseries, *The Old Curiosity Shop*. She is preparing to take part in a workshop production of Thomas Middleton's *The Witch* – one of the plays she is using in her selections from the New Mermaid series and is currently playing 'Lady Catherine de Bourgh' in the stage adaptation of *Pride and Prejudice*.

She is also Co-Director of the Actors' Theatre School and is the author of two books on auditioning and audition technique – *Actors' Audition Speeches for all ages and accents* and *Actresses' Audition Speeches for all ages and accents*. It is her untiring search for suitable audition material for our students, which has inspired this useful collection of classical speeches.

Eamonn Jones
Founder Director
The Actors' Theatre School

CONTENTS

Classical Audition Speeches

Preface

Finding suitable audition speeches is an on-going problem for both students and professional actors alike – particularly when looking for good classical material which has not been over-used. Most students preparing an audition speech for drama school read the word 'classical' in the audition requirements and look no further than Shakespeare. This is an easy option. Local bookshops and libraries usually have a 'Complete Works of Shakespeare', whereas other classical plays are more difficult, or even impossible, to track down at short notice. This is a great pity because, although Shakespeare is undoubtedly our greatest playwright, there is an enormous wealth and variety of other classical work being sadly neglected. Auditioners get tired of listening to the same old pieces being trotted out again and again, and the Royal Academy of Dramatic Art in London have even gone as far as to publish a list of those speeches they simply don't want to hear any more!

In these two books of *Classical Audition Speeches* – one for men and one for women – I have endeavoured to include selections that are not so well known, and perhaps some that may never have been used until now. There are some splendid dramatic opportunities in *The Revenger's Tragedy*, *'Tis Pity She's a Whore*, and *The Duchess of Malfi*, as well as some very funny speeches such as 'Angelica's' in *Love for Love* where she threatens to expose her uncle as a wizard. You will also find a variety of accents, for example 'Margery Pinchwife' in *The Country Wife*. All the selections have been taken from the New Mermaid series of classical plays, and can be found in most bookshops and bigger libraries. Each has an introduction which is very readable and is packed with really useful background information for actors.

All the speeches have been tried and tested by students at the Actors' Theatre School, either in class or in auditions or outside drama examinations – so they really do work!

I hope these books will not only fulfil a need for students and professional actors looking for fresh material, but also provide a quick and handy reference when the telephone rings with that unexpected audition for one of the lesser-known classical plays.

Acknowledgements

I would like to say thank you to the actors, directors, playwrights, casting directors, agents and organisations who have helped me with this book, including:

Michael Attenborough, Nicholas Barter, Richard Carpenter, Frances Cuka, George Cuttingham, Gillian Diamond, Patrick Duggan, Margaret Hamilton, Rona Laurie, Peter Layton, Jacky Leggo, Malcolm Morrison, Sue Parrish, Paul Peters, Keith Salberg, Brian Schwartz, of Offstage Bookshop in London, Don Taylor, Di Trevis, Mervyn Wycherley, Amieth Yogarajah.

And not forgetting my co-director, Eamonn Jones, without whom this book would never have been compiled, and the students themselves who tried out all these audition speeches for me.

Introduction

When I was at school we were forced to study Shakespeare, and later Ben Jonson and Christopher Marlowe. I hated them all. I was sent to elocution classes because I spoke badly. The teacher was a great believer in Shakespeare as a cure for a London accent, and there I was, at the age of twelve, being 'Cleopatra' bitten by an asp, writhing all over her front room carpet, and a most unlikely 'Julius Caesar'. Then came the End of Term Play, and because they knew I was taking elocution classes, I was chosen to play 'Oberon' in *A Midsummer Night's Dream*. I was squeezed into a tight green silk costume that just about covered my podgy figure, and I had to sing:

> I know a bank whereon the wild thyme blows
> Where oxlips and the nodding violet grows . . .

The tune still haunts me. I have a vivid memory of tripping over the uneven green canvas that had been used to cover the school swimming pool as I made my hurried exit, looking more like Toad of Toad Hall than the King of the Fairies.

Scenes like this stick in your mind and it took three years of drama school to overcome an uneasy feeling when anyone mentioned 'the classics'. Some people never recover. I remember one of my first jobs in the theatre where the leading lady had it written into her contract, that whenever the company put on a classical play she had a 'fortnight out'.

This was a long time ago, but the same feeling often prevails today. A sixteen year old student told me he had never studied any Shakespeare. The class had 'voted him out', he said. (Perhaps their parents had had similar experiences to mine.) 'What about the other classics?' I asked. He didn't know. Anyway, they were going to do a modern play instead!

So let's try and clear up a few misconceptions concerning 'the classics'. The word 'classic' according to Webster's Dictionary means 'a work of enduring excellence'. Therefore all the speeches in this book are taken from plays of 'enduring excellence'. They 'endured' because they entertained and enlightened audiences for many years and continue to do so today. They are the very best of their kind and we should be grateful for the opportunity to play them, not see them as some sort of stumbling block.

Recently, a ten year old student of mine went to see a performance of *Dr Faustus* at his big brother's school. 'They had a candle on stage, burning all the way through. That represented Faustus' life,' he said. 'At the end of the play when the devils got him, the candle was blown out and the stage was all dark. It was good. I liked it.' So that school, at least, saw Christopher Marlowe's play as an entertainment, not an academic exercise.

The days of performing 'the classics' in a declamatory style with exaggerated gestures, a pained expression and the 'voice beautiful' are thankfully over. Directors nowadays have very different, and often controversial, ideas on how Shakespeare, Marlowe and Jonson should be played. Barry Rutter, Artistic Director of the Northern Broadsides Company, uses northern actors, thereby celebrating 'the spontaneity, unpredictability and festivity of theatre using classic texts with a coherent voice style firmly rooted in the North of England'. However, I agree with Rona Laurie, who in her recent book, *The Actor's Art and Craft*, said: 'It is important for an actor who wishes to play a range of parts, including classical ones, to have, in addition to any regional accent he may speak, a pure enunciation of vowel sounds . . . '

Many students and professional actors shy away from the classics, imagining that you have to have some sort of academic background in order to play them. In fact it is often better to start from nothing – with no preconceived ideas. The characters in Ben Jonson's *The Alchemist* are 'low life' Londoners. They fight, they lie, they cheat and they steal, and you don't have to be an academic with a 'posh' accent to do that. But you do need, as Barrie Rutter says, 'a coherent voice style'. Your voice has to carry and you have to be heard at the back of the auditorium.

But let's take a look at the first audition most of us encounter when we consider 'going into the theatre' or joining 'the rogues and vagabonds' as the Elizabethans might term it – the drama school audition.

Applying and Auditioning for Drama School

You want to become an actor and you've decided, quite rightly in most cases, that the best way to go about it is to apply for Drama School. Twenty or thirty years ago you might have been able to 'get a start' in one of the smaller theatre companies as an 'ASM playing small parts', that is an Assistant Stage Manager, prompting, helping out backstage generally, playing the odd parts of maid, butler or policeman as they came up, and hopefully learning your job that way. But today, with fewer theatres available and most of those unwilling, or unable to take on extra staff, it is most unlikely that you'd even be considered. And writing to fringe theatre trying to get the odd line or two, or working as an extra in films and television, is not going to do you much good. Of course there are young people who are 'discovered' and never went to drama school or had an acting lesson in their lives. They were lucky, if you can call it that. And you can't run your life on luck. The theatre is a precarious business and you've got to give yourself the best possible chance in order to succeed.

Now you've contacted the various schools and asked them to send you a prospectus and application form. The prospectus should outline the courses offered and explain what will be required of you at your audition. Drama courses in Great Britain can be very expensive and it is best to make absolutely sure you can afford the school of your choice before sending off your form and audition fee. Not all local councils, or in the case of students from overseas, governments, are prepared to assist these days. One student was told by his council that they could train five engineers with the money it takes to send a single actor to drama school. Never mind – a few drama schools are now offering degree courses (BA Drama), and councils are inclined to look more favourably on these. You will also find some universities offering drama courses, but these tend to be more academic.

In the United States there are very few vocational drama schools such as the Royal Academy of Dramatic Art (RADA) or the Guildhall School of Music and Drama in London. The equivalent would be the American Academy of Dramatic Arts or the Juilliard School in New York. Most drama courses are affiliated to universities, such as Yale, and are again very expensive. There are no grants available, but you may qualify for a student loan. If you elect to go to drama school there are scholarships you can apply for, or you could approach one of the various Foundations (i.e. organisations or trusts), such as the Carnegie-Mellon Foundation, for a theatre bursary or scholarship. When you have selected the school that has the most to offer you and have sent in your fee and application form, do make sure you have read the audition requirements thoroughly. You really should apply for more than one school as you rarely get accepted on a first audition, although it has been known. Classical speeches in particular get better the more they are performed and there is no doubt about it, you develop a way of handling auditions. At your second attempt you will not be nearly so nervous and you will begin to look around you and compare notes with others who are experiencing the same thing as yourself. Your first couple of auditions should, I think, be treated as a learning process.

Most schools require you to perform two contrasting speeches of about three minutes each, one modern and one classical, often stipulating that the classical speech must be in verse. Sometimes you are asked to prepare a song and given some movement and improvisation to do. A few schools ask for three prepared speeches, although they may not even ask to hear the third, and others send out a list of about ten selections, ask you to pick out one or sometimes two of them, and then contrast these with a piece of your own choice. All speeches and the song must be learnt by heart. It is surprising how many would-be drama students think all they have to do is just stand up and read everything!

Choosing a suitable audition piece

Whether you are choosing a classical or modern speech, it is best to find a part that is near to your own age and experience, unless of course you have a particular talent or liking for playing older or younger parts convincingly.

Do make sure that you read the audition requirements *carefully*, particularly with regard to your classical speech. Sometimes you

4

may be given two or even three periods to choose from. There is no point in picking out a speech from a Restoration comedy that you rather like, if they have asked for something from an Elizabethan or Jacobean drama, written in blank verse.

The speeches in this book are mainly from plays written in the following periods:

Elizabethan (1558–1603)
Including, among others, speeches from the tragedies, *Arden of Faversham, Edward the Second* and the comedy *The Shoemaker's Holiday*. All selections are in verse.

Jacobean (1603–1625)
Including selections from *The Duchess of Malfi, The Revenger's Tragedy, Bartholmew Fair* and *Eastward Ho!*. Again the majority of these are written in verse, with the exception of the last two comedies mentioned, which are in prose.

Restoration (1660–1710)
This is the period following Charles II's return from France – the Restoration of the Monarchy – and for the first time in England actresses appeared on stage. The speeches included are mostly taken from Restoration comedies such as *The Way of the World* and *The Relapse* and are written in prose, the notable exception being Dryden's tragedy, *All for Love* which is written in blank verse.

Late Eighteenth Century
Including speeches from such comedies as *The Rivals* and *The School for Scandal* – all written in prose.

Late Nineteenth Century
Including speeches from the comedies of Oscar Wilde, such as *The Importance of Being Earnest* and *Lady Windermere's Fan*. All written in prose.

Contrast

Contrast is an important word in the theatre. Contrast keeps an audience from becoming bored – and an auditioner too. Look at those audition requirements and you will see the word 'contrast'.

Contrast your speeches. If you have already selected something dramatic, contrast it with a comedy, or try something with a different accent. Shakespeare is, as I have already said, our greatest playwright, but it is good to ring the changes sometimes and look further afield. In America they lay less emphasis on Shakespeare and encourage students to look at work by some of his contemporaries as well.

The Drama Centre London, one of the schools that send out a list of classical speeches to choose from, included selections from John Ford's *'Tis Pity She's a Whore* last season. A German student of mine gained a place at Drama Centre with 'Giovanni's' opening speech from *'Tis Pity She's a Whore*, contrasting it with a modern piece from a Neil Simon play. And an Italian student used 'Hippolita's' speech from the same Ford play, contrasting it with a speech from a Dario Fo play and won a place at the E15 Acting School. Both classical speeches are included in these books.

Preparation

If you look at the front of this book you will see that I have dedicated it to Thomas Dogget (1670–1721) – a fine actor and famous as a 'low comedian'. It is said that at the age of twenty-five he took lodgings in Wapping in order to prepare himself for his role as the sailor, 'Ben', in *Love for Love* – a part written especially for him by the playwright William Congreve. Other actors in this comedy, which opened at the new playhouse in Lincoln's Inn Fields, London, included Thomas Betterton and the great Elizabeth Barry, but it was Dogget who was considered to be the greatest success of the production. How many young or, for that matter, older actors would go to that much trouble to perfect a part? He was extremely popular as an all-round entertainer – he could also sing – and was perhaps a Max Wall or Jimmy Jewell of his time. Thirteen years later he played the foolish old knight, 'Sir Paul Plyant', in Congreve's *The Double-Dealer* and was mentioned for his 'Unparrell'd' performance.

Read the Play

The very first step in your preparation is to read the play. I cannot overemphasise the importance of this. You owe it to the playwright and you owe it to yourself. Many students simply cannot see the point of this, particularly as they are only preparing one speech, not performing in the whole play. The point is that you need to know whom you are talking to in this particular speech. 'Does it matter?' one student said to me. Of course it matters. It matters very much indeed. Your attitude to the character or characters you are speaking to alters according to the sort of people they are, their motives and your motives for speaking to them. Are they friends or enemies? People you love, people you hate, or people you are indifferent to? What has happened in the previous scene? What has just been said that makes you react in a particular way? Is your speech in answer to a question? If you don't know the question, how can you possibly answer?

'Tamyra's' speech in *Bussy D'Ambois* begins:

> Farewell, my light and life. But not in him,
> [In mine own dark love and light bent to another.]

Who is she saying farewell to? And who is the other man – the 'another'? I have given the answers in the introduction to this speech, but that is not nearly enough information. 'Tamyra's' emotions are extremely complex and her character, and the character and emotions of her husband and lover have to be thoroughly understood. You need to read and reread the play. Gather as much information as you can about your character and ask yourself:

1. What does your character say or think about herself?
2. What does she say or think about the other characters in the play?
3. What do they say or think about her?
4. What has happened in the previous scene?
5. What does your character want?
   (a) In this particular scene?
   (b) Throughout the play?
6. What is the playwright's intention in this scene? Are we meant to laugh or cry?
7. Each character is making a journey. At what stage in the journey are you when you are performing this speech?

Sometimes, of course, the information given in the play is insufficient and you need to look further. 'Mistress Otter' in *Epicoene* is described as an Amazonian china-woman. What is a china-woman? It certainly doesn't mean she comes from China, and it's important to find out more about it.

Try to discover as much as you can about the period the play is written in and what was the social and political situation at that time.

All the above information is essential to the process of building up your character.

Language

Classical plays tend to be written in heightened language and often, as in the case of the Elizabethan and Jacobean period, in blank verse. And so we need to learn and practise additional skills in order to perform them so that an audience can both hear and understand us.

Blank verse means verse that does not rhyme, but has a recognisable rhythm – and fortunately the rhythm used by most playwrights in this period is the one we use now in everyday speech. It is the measure, pulse or pattern most natural to the English language; an unstressed syllable followed by a stressed syllable. When actors understand this, they find speaking in blank verse very much easier than they thought, and realise they don't need to declaim it in tortured tones or stand up and recite it like a poem. The speeches in this collection come from plays, and plays are meant to be acted not 'speechified'.

You will hear people talk of the metre of verse and I think it's important for actors to know at least something about this. Metre is simply the 'grammar of rhythm' or, in other words, how the rhythm is technically described. Blank verse is usually written in 'five foot iambic metre'. Such a line consists of five 'feet'. Each *iambic* foot is a pair of syllables where the first syllable is unstressed, the second stressed. Each iambic foot is written like this: ⌣—. And so a regular line of blank verse can be written:

⌣—/⌣—/⌣—/⌣—/⌣—

We would write down a single line of verse from the 'Duchess of Malfi's' speech like this:

In my / last will / I have / not much / to give
⌣ — / ⌣ — / ⌣ — / ⌣ — / ⌣ —

However, if we followed this metre exactly it would sound like a child reciting:

de dum / de dum / de dum / de dum / de dum

So now we have to place the stresses so that the line makes sense while not disrupting the structure of the verse. An actress playing the 'Duchess of Malfi' might well stress the words 'last' and 'will' equally, in order to make better sense of the line and also to make it sound more natural. This is, of course, a matter for individual choice.

Not every line of blank verse is regular and it is the irregularities that give interest and very often a clue to how the playwright intended a line to be said. Frequently you find a heavy stress at the beginning of a line, sometimes an extra unstressed syllable at the end, occasionally a line that is very short indeed.

There are many instances in blank verse where there is no punctuation at the end of a line and you need to read straight on to the next line until it makes sense, as for example at the beginning of the 'Duchess's' speech from *The Revenger's Tragedy*:

Was't ever known step-duchess was so mild
And calm as I? Some now would plot his death
With easy doctors . . .

It is usual for the voice to rise/or inflect upwards where the sentence or thought is incomplete, and downwards where the thought or sentence is completed. You do this in modern English. In both the first and second lines of this speech the thought or sense carries over to the following line. And so you need to have an upward inflection at the end to indicate that the sense runs on, and also a very slight pause to show that it is the end of a verse line – again we have to be careful not to spoil the structure of the verse.

Most people agree that you should not take a breath at the end of a line where the sense runs on, but there are of course exceptions to this rule, depending sometimes on a particular characterisation or mood, and often on the director's own ideas on the subject!

When another character's line or lines have been deleted in a speech written in verse, as in Hecate's speech from *The Witch*,

I have indicated where 'Sebastian's' line ('Can there be such things done?') is cut, as follows:

> ... Are these the skins
> Of serpents? these of snakes?

The first part of the verse line is obviously missing and you need to be aware of this and compensate with a pause, or perhaps a move as Hecate indicates, or show Sebastian the skins.

Not all Elizabethan and Jacobean speeches are written in verse. The speeches from *Bartholmew Fair* are all in prose, and even in most of the verse plays the comedians and 'low life' characters usually speak prose. 'Sybil's' speech from *The Shoemaker's Holiday* is written in both verse and prose.

As we move into the Restoration period (1660–1710), the popular comedies of the day, such as *Love for Love* and *The Way of the World*, are written in prose, but their exuberant and often flamboyant style needs considerable vocal technique, as do the plays of the late eighteenth and nineteenth centuries. Long lines and extended images demand good breath control at the very least.

Words

Very often if you speak words you are unfamiliar with it can get in the way of your performance. You feel unnatural saying them and it shows. Another good reason for reading the play! Most editions, certainly the New Mermaid series of classical plays, give meanings of words and expressions that you wouldn't normally find in your dictionary, and you need to keep practising these until they roll easily off the tongue. Expletives such as 'Slight', 'Sdeath' and 'Slid' – meaning 'God's light', 'God's death' and 'God's eyelid' – are particularly difficult to cope with. My student, Jenny, was performing 'Dol Common's' speech from *The Alchemist* and found 'Sdeath' almost an impossibility. So we changed it to 'God!' until she got used to the run of the line, and then she found she was easily able to cope with the original 'Sdeath!' Improvisation can be of great help here, and it can be useful to try putting the speech into your own words.

Voice and Speech

Many people imagine that voice and speech are one and the same thing. They are not. Voice is the sound we make and speech is the way in which we shape that sound in order to communicate with others. Whether performing in a modern or a classical play the most important thing is for an actor to be clearly heard. I remember seeing a final year production at one of the bigger drama schools and I found one of the players extremely difficult to hear. When I commented on this afterwards, I was told it didn't matter because 'she'd be doing television'. Even on television you need a certain degree of clarity and the sound man often has to tell an actor to 'speak up!' or give him 'a bit more voice'.

Obviously classical speeches put extra demands on the voice. You need good vocal control to manage two, and sometimes three, lines of verse on one breath, or convey extended images of thought without chopping up or losing the sense. Ends of words also need to be considered – 't' and 'd' must not be missed off – and 'street cred' is definitely out.

A voice needs to be taken care of and exercised daily. No ballet dancer would dream of going on stage without some sort of 'warm-up' or exercise, so why should it be any different for an actor? There is not enough space here to outline voice and speech routines, but I would advise you to work on a few simple breathing exercises each day, together with perhaps a few 'tongue twisters' to firm up the beginnings and ends of your words. Malcolm Morrison in his excellent book, *Classical Acting*, gives some good basic exercises, but he also comments that although there are many good books on voice and speech, 'these do not replace work done with a good teacher'.

Movement

It is important to move well and with confidence on stage, but it is also important to consider the period your character is from. Movement is affected by costume. For example, what sort of shoes is your character wearing? They will certainly affect your walk.

Your movement will also be affected by the costume of the period, whether it be: farthingales, petticoats and the weight of heavily brocaded materials in the overskirts of the Elizabethan ladies; the hoops and crinolines of the mid-Victorian period; or the bustles that moved in and out of fashion up to and including Edwardian times. Have a look at costume books and study the paintings of perhaps the Restoration period. Notice how the upper part of the body is carried very straight, as bodices were tight and restricting. The shoulders were bare, with tight three-quarter length sleeves showing the lower arm framed by a fall of lace. The gestures would therefore tend to be wide – with no jerky modern movements. Shoes were high-heeled and the ball of the foot was placed down before the heel when walking.

It is interesting to note that even in 1592 actors were warned against unnecessary movements '... And this I bar, over and besides, that none of you stroke your beards to make action, play with your cod-piece points, or stand fumbling on your buttons when you know not how to bestow your fingers.' Thomas Nashe. I wonder what advice he would have given to actresses, had there been any around in those days!

Of course Thomas Nashe was referring to fidgeting on stage, and often today you see students standing like sticks, arms straight at their sides, clenching and unclenching their hands while they deliver their speech. There is also the temptation among the more confident, to overdo movement and gesture, waving the arms about in a supposedly Elizabethan, Restoration or Victorian manner. Let's face it, we're talking about a three minute audition speech. If you used the proportionate amount of gesture throughout the whole play, you'd be flailing about like a windmill all evening. Every movement and gesture should be properly motivated. A good motto might be, 'When in doubt leave it out'.

What do I wear at the audition?

Most schools will tell you what to wear at your audition, particularly if they are starting with some sort of warm-up or movement session. The main thing is to be comfortable. If you know there is going to be movement and improvisation, wear something casual – tights, trousers and jazz shoes (the ones with the small heels) are easy to work in. It is best to put on a long practice skirt for classical speeches. You can always slip it on over your other clothes. It makes the appropriate movement easier, and prevents you from taking great long strides, as we all tend to do when we wear trousers. You might even take along an extra pair of shoes with heels of the particular period. I think dressing in black looks good at this sort of audition, and you can always add on or take off the 'extra bits' for your second or third speech.

If the speech is too long

The majority of speeches in this book are between three and four minutes in length – an acceptable time for most auditions. However, there are occasions when you are specifically required to limit your time to two or even one and a half minutes. If you go over this time you are liable to be stopped before you get to the end, and if you rush it you will spoil your performance. Be bold. Cut it down to the required length. This is not nearly as difficult as it might seem. For instance 'Angelica's' speech from *Love for Love* can be cut considerably by finishing on '. . . or at least making a voyage to Greenland to inhabit there all the dark season'. And 'Hippolita's' speech from *'Tis Pity She's a Whore* finishes very neatly on the line:

Doth loathe the memory of what is past.

If the speech cannot be reduced easily, or you feel by cutting it you will lose sense or quality, have a look through the play. The character may well have another speech lasting only a minute and a half.

Should you have coaching?

A lot of drama schools say they don't want to see a carefully drilled performance and I agree with them. However, I do think you need some help and advice from a trusted, experienced actor or teacher. A few tips on 'voice' and the 'speaking of blank verse' certainly wouldn't go amiss. For instance, a student came to see me, having carefully re-typed her classical audition speech from blank verse into prose. She proudly handed me half a dozen copies saying, 'These should be useful for you and so much easier to read'.

I hope what I have said in these pages has been helpful and not too daunting. As you can see, classical speeches need a lot of extra work. But if in doubt – concentrate on the acting. Remember a drama school is looking for potential, not perfection.

George Cuttingham

I asked George Cuttingham, President of the American Academy of Dramatic Arts, in New York, to give a few words of advice to students performing classical speeches for the first time:

> At the American Academy of Dramatic Arts, we see classical material as presenting the actor with a dual challenge: to speak lines that are far removed from everyday conversation (lines that are often rich with wit and poetic imagery and seething with exalted emotion), and to do so with the same quality of honest, personal connection – to the dramatic circumstance, to one's own feelings and to other actors – that is desirable when acting simple contemporary material.
>
> While untrained actors will not usually have the vocal development and verbal skills to do full justice to classical material, they can still audition effectively if they speak the lines clearly and simply, without indicating emotion they do not feel, remembering that the character is a human being with something to say and a reason for saying it, not someone intent on demonstrating perfect vowel sounds.

Nicholas Barter

Nicholas Barter, Principal of The Royal Academy of Dramatic Art in London, had this to say:

> The Royal Academy of Dramatic Art (RADA) auditions between 1400 and 1500 students a year for 30 available places.
>
> Applicants are required to present a contrasting classical speech and a modern speech. With so many auditioning it is always advisable to avoid speeches which the audition panel sees over and over again. Try to find a classical piece that suits your age and temperament. Make sure you read the whole play so that you know the context of the scene and be prepared to look outside the better known Shakespeare speeches when preparing something from the sixteenth or seventeenth centuries. Learn the speech thoroughly, making sure you understand the meaning of every word and the kind of character you are playing. Above all, make it real and truthful.

Rona Laurie

And finally, Rona Laurie, ex-actress, well-known drama coach and experienced auditioner, has this to say about the importance of choosing good material:

Both the winner and runner-up in this year's Drama Student of the Year Competition sponsored by *The Stage* and *Theatre World* chose classical speeches to perform in the final. Very few of the twenty-six actors competing in the preceding round at Wembley Exhibition Centre had gone to Elizabethan and Jacobean plays for their choice. As one of the panel of three judges I had no doubt in my mind of the advantage that their choice of classical speeches had given the two successful students. There were, I believe, three main reasons.

First, of course, the quality and power of the language, secondly the dramatic impact of the playwrights' creation of situation and, thirdly, the fact that the speeches came so freshly to the ears of a panel long-accustomed to a repetitive repertoire of over-used audition speeches from modern plays, and not always the best plays available.

My advice to anyone looking for audition material would be to search for the best plays of their kind. Several of the performers we saw obviously had promise but failed to rise above the poor quality of their speeches.

In the field of classical drama, particularly in the Elizabethan and Jacobean periods there is still a wealth of exciting, comparatively unused material to be found.

Auditioning for Professional Theatre

After completing drama school you will continue to audition in some form or other throughout your career, even if it is only an 'interview' with perhaps an invitation to 'come in and read the script'. However, if you have had: some solid stage training; have worked on your voice and movement; have had the opportunity of developing various characters and learning to play opposite other actors without 'falling over the furniture', you stand a better chance of gaining professional employment and staying in the 'business'. Even from a practical point of view, at the end of your drama school training you will be performing in front of agents and casting directors in your final productions, and you will stand a chance of being selected for representation or be given the opportunity of auditioning for a professional theatre company. For those who are thinking in terms of films and television only, I would mention that you usually come by this sort of work because someone has seen you performing on stage in the first place. Very few film and television directors are going to take a risk on casting a young actor or actress with no professional experience whatsoever, and the best way to gain this experience is in the theatre.

'Getting a start' can be a major problem, but by now you should have a fairly wide range of audition speeches, gathered together over your two or three years as a student.

Your very first audition could well be for a repertory or a summer stock company (if you are in the United States), where a different play is presented every two or three weeks, sometimes monthly and in a few rare exceptions these days, weekly. I spoke to Agent and Personal Manager, Jacky Leggo who had this to say:

> Most theatre companies ask for one classical and one modern piece to be prepared when auditioning. It is very useful to be able to refer to a choice of classical speeches in one book, as very often these auditions are arranged at short notice, leaving an artiste little research time. Many people choose Shakespearian speeches when asked for something classical,

16

but it is important to have a varied choice, to avoid a Director hearing the same pieces over and over again.

Try to find out what plays are listed for the season, and use speeches that are appropriate, especially for your classic selection. If you know they are putting on an Oscar Wilde play there is not much point in presenting a piece from a Jacobean revenge play. If you are auditioning for a company presenting plays in repertoire, i.e. a company which performs a number of plays, rotating them regularly, then the same thing applies. London, of course, capitalises on this system with the Royal National Theatre and Royal Shakespeare companies planning their programmes so that tourists and visitors can see as many as four plays within a fortnight.

Be warned! It is important to keep your audition selections 'brushed-up' – or at least go over the words every now and then. As Jacky Leggo has already confirmed, many of these companies expect actors to be able to audition at a moment's notice. Recently a company auditioning for 'Phaedra' expected a piece of Greek tragedy prepared within forty-eight hours, and it's not unknown for a certain well-known company to ring up actors the night before and ask them to bring a piece of verse from one of the classics to perform the following morning! It is also a good idea to refresh your memory about 'language' (see page 8). It's only too easy when you are called to a last minute audition, to hastily revise a piece of classical verse, forgetting that it *is* verse, ignoring the rhythm and where the breaths should come, and turn it into a piece of prose. I know, I've done it myself!

Frequently an actor or actress is asked to audition for one specific part in a particular production. It could be a tour, a play coming into the West End of London, or in the States – a Broadway or off-Broadway production. This is an entirely different sort of audition, where suitability often counts more than capability. You are not likely to be asked to play 'Mrs Hardcastle' in *She Stoops to Conquer* if you are in your early twenties or 'Ursla' the pig-woman in *Bartholmew Fair* unless you are fairly plump! You will most certainly be asked to read or sight-read and will be judged initially on your suitability for the part, i.e. age, appearance, build, voice-range, etc.

A word about reading or sight-reading

In theatre, films, television and radio, being asked to read or sight-read for a part are one and the same thing. It means that you will be given a script to read that you have never seen before and be expected to give some sort of reasonable performance, or at least a good indication of how you would play the part. You may be given a few minutes to look through it, but sometimes you only have time for a quick glance and then have to begin reading. You should try to look up from the page as much as possible, so that the auditioner can see your face and also so that the words are 'lifted' from the page, rather than looking down all the time and mumbling into your script. Sight-reading is a skill that can be learnt and practised until you can eventually hold a line, or part of a line, in your head and look up where appropriate, instead of being hampered by having to look down all the time. If you are asked to read blank verse don't let yourself be panicked and don't be rushed into your reading. Ask if you can have a couple of minutes to look through it. Glance down the right-hand side of the verse lines and note where there is no punctuation at the end of line and the sense runs over to the next line, so that you can make sure that you don't take a breath at that point. Take your time. If some of the words are unknown to you or difficult to pronounce, don't stop or say 'sorry', just carry on with confidence. Sometimes verse is easier to read than prose, as you'll find you can retain more of it in 'your mind's eye'.

Fringe theatre in this country, and off off-Broadway in the United States, has proliferated as many commercial and subsidised companies have had to close down. Most of these operate in pub theatres or in small arts centres. Several are experimental and of a very high standard indeed, but unfortunately not well funded, and 'profit share' has become a euphemism, with rare exceptions, for 'no money for the cast' or 'expenses only'. However, it gives actors who are not working a chance to be seen by directors and casting directors, and there is considerable competition for some of the better parts. Mostly, as in paid theatre, you will be required to read and sometimes asked to prepare a modern or classical speech. Some excellent classic plays are produced on the fringe, *Love for Love* is being performed as I write this, and it can be one of the best ways of gaining experience and adding to your C.V.

Advice from the actors

I spoke to two well-known actors, who have performed in some of the plays from which these speeches were taken, and asked them if they could give some tips and advice on auditioning for classic plays, and perhaps tell us a little about their own experience on these occasions.

Patrick Duggan

Irish actor, Patrick Duggan, who trained at the Dublin Gate Theatre with the Edwards MacLiammoir Company, was recently in the West End production of *Philadelphia, Here I Come!*, played 'Father Murphy' in the television comedy series, *The Upper Hand* and is currently appearing in BBC Television's *EastEnders*, had this to say:

> Reading for a part in a classic presents difficulties not found in doing so for a part in a modern play. The strangeness of the language and the lack of familiar terms of reference can prevent quick characterisation.
>
> I encountered these difficulties in abundance when asked by director Stephen Unwin to read for the part of 'Foigard' in the English Touring Theatre's production of *The Beaux' Stratagem* by George Farquhar. 'Foigard' is an Irish cleric, who for reasons never made quite clear, is pretending to be Belgian. His dialogue is an almost crazed mixture of stage-Irish and stage-continental. Halfway through my reading I stopped and asked if I was on the right track.
>
> > 'It's wonderful,' said Stephen.
> > 'Don't get carried away,' I said to myself.
> > '"Wonderful" doesn't necessarily mean you've got the part!'
>
> I think that one should not be afraid to ask a director such a question, nor to reread a line or passage if not satisfied with one's rendering. There is no reason for an audition to be a shot in the dark. Speak up!
>
> For the record ... in this case 'Wonderful' did mean I got the part.
>
> When I read for the part of 'Philly Cullen' in Lindsay Anderson's production of Synge's *Playboy of the Western World* I felt on very certain ground indeed.

19

I had played the part twice before, on radio and on the stage, so I was very familiar with Synge's heightened version of Irish speech. Also, being Irish myself the accent presented no problem. Not that accent need present a problem. Many actors and actresses are obsessed with getting an accent right. Often at the expense of believable characterisation and the suppression of personality. I believe that it is much more important to produce the cadences of an accent than to waste time trying for what, in fact, can never sound 'authentic', for the simple reason that it is not.

Lindsay Anderson was not impressed by my genuine authenticity . . . he didn't give me the part. So there!

Frances Cuka

Then I spoke to Frances Cuka, a Royal Shakespeare and Royal National Theatre player, working in this country and in the States, who made her name as 'Jo' in *A Taste of Honey* in the West End and more recently played 'Mrs Nickleby' in *Nicholas Nickleby* on Broadway, and 'Mrs Dudgeon' in the Royal National Theatre's *The Devil's Disciple*.

When I was a lot younger I went up for a part in a Restoration comedy, for one of those saucy maid's parts, knowing, witty and sexy, who usually wears a dress cut down to the nipples. I knew the director and knew he liked my work. After the audition I had a rather smart lunch date, so I had gone along wearing my best black suit and high-heeled shoes. My director friend looked stricken. 'Can you come back in a couple of days' time, wearing something more suitable?' he asked. – Two days later I returned, this time wearing a full skirt, low-necked blouse and a belt that nipped me in at the waist. I read for him and got the job.

Another director friend, considered very avant-garde in his day, once told me that when he was casting a period play he would never consider any girl who turned up wearing jeans and a T-shirt. Psychologically he found it rather insulting to himself, he felt it showed arrogance, and/or sloppiness on the actress's part and made his job of ascertaining her worth more difficult. Both directors were men of imagination and fanatical attention to detail. Striking a wrong note as you walk in the door can seriously hamper your chance of getting the part.

Work on your voice; the dialogue can be deceptively simple, sometimes convoluted, but there should be a naturalness about the delivery, and good diction is essential. If you have done the very best you can, you still may not get the job, because the director didn't think you were quite suitable, but he or she may remember you for another production later.

When you do a Restoration play you go back in time, in dress and dialogue, but not in humanity. There are real people under those periwigs. They may be greedy, sex-obsessed and bitchy, so what's new? My favourite character is all of these things. 'Lady Wishfort' in *The Way of the World* is a domestic tyrant who forbids her niece to marry the man she loves, because 'Lady Wishfort' fancies him herself. Laughed at and plotted against by the younger people for being a widow of fifty-five still on the lookout for a man, 'Lady Wishfort' ploughs through the play like a great battleship, past her prime but indomitable, trailing streamers of glory. Her rages are tremendous – 'Ods my life, I'll have him. I'll have him murdered. I'll have him poisoned. Where does he eat?' – and topical – 'I warrant the spendthrift-prodigal's in debt as much as a million lottery, or the whole court upon a birthday.' After this rage has subsided, her make-up has cracked and needs repairing. 'I look like an old peeled wall.' 'Foible', her maid, busy repairing the damage observes, 'A little art once made your picture like you, and now a little of the same art must make you like your picture. Your picture must sit for you, Madam.' Aah – it comes to us all in the end. Yet her recklessness and lust for life sustain her. At the end of the play, when all the plots against her have been revealed, she accepts defeat with dignity, though I'm not so sure that she won't be on the rampage a week or so later. If you look at the cast list of *The Way of the World* there are an equal number of men and women, six parts each and that's missing out two women, 'Betty' and 'Peg', both small parts.

Restoration plays show a good ratio of women's parts, good women's parts, and for a very good reason. When the Monarchy was restored, so was the theatre – under the Parliamentarians everything that was enjoyable was a sin, and the theatres, being thoroughly sinful, were closed down. Now they were open for business again with a new novelty guaranteed to pull in the punters. Instead of boys there were real women playing the women's parts! And the public flocked to see this new phenomenon. The playwrights responded with a cornucopia of lovely ladies – randy, argumentative, bitchy,

21

conniving, mincing (the name of a maid in *The Way of the World*), flouncing and strutting, women in breeches, even a female Casanova who fought duels. So when you audition for one of these feisty beings you can't be a shy violet. Even the Goody-two-Shoes, the friend of the heroine and the second love interest, is intelligent and witty and a better part than you get in most modern plays. You mustn't slouch – those ladies with their low-necked dresses and laced-in waists knew they were being looked over, and flaunted what they'd got. They arrived on the stage, never to depart, and they knew their value. Try to read these plays as they read them, new and exciting and fresh, not some old play that's been around for donkey's years. The gold's still there – it's up to you to make it glitter.

What directors and casting directors look for

What are auditioners looking for when they ask you to prepare a classical speech or invite you to audition for a specific part in an Elizabethan, Jacobean, Restoration or late eighteenth- or nineteenth-century play?

Gillian Diamond

I spoke to Gillian Diamond – Head of Casting with the Royal National Theatre for fifteen years and also the Royal Shakespeare Company, and now Associate Producer for the Sir Peter Hall Company – who runs a course at the Drama Centre, preparing third year students for entry into the profession – and she had this to say:

> For general auditions, read the play carefully and choose wisely to suit your character and your strengths. Try to be original. If it is a piece of verse you have been asked for, use the verse properly, don't make it into prose. Always have a variety of pieces and keep changing them, they quickly become stale and therefore uninteresting. If you are liked, you may be asked to do something else. Make sure you have a choice to offer up.
>
> Be imaginative; create the character and set your scene. Find the style of your piece, particularly in something like Oscar Wilde or a late eighteenth-century play, in order to assist the director or casting director to visualise you in the period

of the piece. Always imagine the person you are talking to in the scene and place them so that they become a reality for you, and therefore for the director. Never talk directly to your audience unless you decide on a soliloquy. If you don't like the way you have started, you can always stop and start again.

Wear clothes to assist your character and chuck the trainers.

If you know what play is being cast you could choose a piece written in a similar style and period. You could also choose a character that has similarities. You can never be too well prepared. Don't plead lack of time, or lack of being informed as an excuse; it may be true, but nobody really cares. Most of the people you will meet are nice and wish you to succeed, so meet them with a positive attitude. Never be grim. Try to be well informed and enthusiastic about the profession.

Remember that 'many are called and few are chosen.' All you can do is to come out knowing you have done your best – no regrets.

Di Trevis

Di Trevis has directed for the Royal Shakespeare Company, the Royal National Theatre and the Royal Opera House and has run professional workshops at the Riverside Studios, London, and in France and Germany. In 1987, she directed *The Revenger's Tragedy* at the Swan Theatre in Stratford and later at the Barbican with Antony Sher in the leading role:

Let's face it. Auditioning is asking someone to love you. And they often say no. Think about this now and decide how you are going to deal with it.

Directors ask actors to perform classical pieces, such as you will find in this book, precisely because they are very difficult. Such a text will usually be of assured quality, will not yield to superficial work, and will require a mixture of technical skills in speaking, understanding and communicating. Choose a piece for which you have a real affinity, one that stimulates your imagination and fills you with a feeling for the character: words you want to say. What you should aim to bring to the piece is truth, your own intuition of the character's feelings drawn from a unique experience. Yours. This will make the practised reading of the speech special and personal.

Firstly, get hold of the play from which the speech is drawn and read the whole play carefully with a pencil in your hand. Write down everything said about the character and everything the character says about him or herself. Look up unusual words in a good dictionary which notes changes of definition at different dates. You will be amazed how words change their meanings over time. A key word written three or four centuries ago might have had quite a different resonance then.

It is part of the fascination of classical work to mine for these subtleties. Work out exactly what is being said. Then spend at least three hours actually speaking the words out loud. This seems simple until you actually do it. It is exhausting. Be careful – you must work in such a way that the words sound as if you just thought of them. This is language that needs practice and yet must never become automatic. Act out all the images until you can really see, feel and **smell** them. Say the speech in your own words. Find equivalent modern day expressions and alternate between your words and the text. Try singing the speech. Take your character out onto the streets or on a Tube journey. How would they react? If a prop is involved, never mime it. It will inform the whole speech. Find, borrow or make a substitute. Take it with you to the audition. Analyse the situation of your character previous to the speech: fighting a duel, riding a horse, hiding in a cupboard. Do it. Note all that has happened to clothes, voice, stance, mood. Get another actor to improvise with you if necessary. All this will bring a vigour and vividness to your work, a general impression of readiness of response, of fresh unblocked energy.

Even your manner of walking through the door of the interview room will be informed by proper preparation. Directors often talk of 'knowing' the moment an actor walks through the door. This is an illusion. But if an actor walks through the door with an air of readiness and an appetite to show you what he has prepared, it makes a far better impression than someone with a set of excuses lingering in the back of his mind.

Nowadays directors often like to work on a speech with the actor, suggest a new approach or ask them to use the text in a different way. If you prepare in the way I suggest you will be able to encompass new ideas, since your own work will have been through many stages and changes.

Nerves? Try improvising ahead of time a person who is calm. This helps enormously. I do it every time I face the first day in a rehearsal room. Ever thought the director might be nervous? They often are. Try putting them at their ease. Have some questions to ask – simple, practical, un-show-offy. It should be a two-way conversation. Face them calmly. Let them look at you. Breathe. Take your time to start the speech, and start again if you feel it's gone disastrously wrong. I find a false start can often be as interesting as the thing itself. When the interview is over, say goodbye cleanly and go. Actors often seem unable to leave and linger ingratiatingly, or seem to be waiting for a word or sign that one is unable to give. This always makes me sad.

An actor's life is mainly trying for jobs. It's rarely getting them. If you do, then the real horror starts: how to play the part!

Malcolm Morrison

Malcolm Morrison is Director of the Theatre Division at the Hartt School, University of Hartford, Connecticut. He is Director of the World Theatre Training Institute and Artistic Director of the Northern Stage Company. He has directed a wide range of classical plays including, most recently, *The Importance of Being Earnest*, *The Beaux' Stratagem* and *The Critic*. He lectures frequently throughout the world. His latest book, *Classical Acting*, has just been published by A & C Black in the UK.

After sitting through many auditions to find actors for classical plays I have come to the conclusion that there is one major concern in making the audition a success and that is – the ability to act. All the grooming, avoidance of 'over-done' material, expensive photographs and handsome résumés are, ultimately, no substitute for the ability to transform the audition space with well chosen material that is deeply understood and executed with a fine, but unobtrusive, technique.

I have been offered lollipops, listened to hard luck stories and, in one case, threatened by a fifty-three year old actor with dyed blue-black hair and eyebrows – 'It's Mercutio or nothing!' he said, with both hands on the table and his face half an inch from mine. But the fact was that none of them could act.

The approach to the works of Oscar Wilde, Bernard Shaw, Shakespeare, or Molière, or any of the other 'greats' of classical literature, should be just as specific and detailed in characterisation and context as to any modern realistic piece. A cursory knowledge of the play, a superficial understanding of the character and an assumed attitude and voice just don't cut it. The temptation to 'play attitude' rather than the character is seductive and has to be avoided; instead there should be detailed, careful work. For example in any of the plays of Oscar Wilde the urge to play a generalised 'Upper Class English' and ignore the social context and the ability to speak long, well-constructed sentences, while maintaining a defined character, is too prevalent.

For what it's worth, my advice is: develop a strong, discreet technique, invest in the character and the play and don't offer lollipops!

Sue Parrish

Sue Parrish is Artistic Director of the Sphinx Theatre Company and Founder Director of the Women's Playhouse Trust. She won Drama Award For Best Production with Penny Casdagli's *Pardon Mr Punch*, and has also directed *The Way of the World* and *The Provoked Wife*. She had this to say about playing Restoration comedy:

The most serious problem facing an actor in approaching these unjustly neglected and glorious plays is their unfamiliarity. Not only are the plays rarely performed but their world is also obscure, overshadowed by the proximity of the Elizabethan and Jacobean period.

So, in taking on a speech from a Restoration comedy, background research is vital in finding the true style. It is important to realise, for example, that the theatres had been closed for eighteen years under the Commonwealth, and, on the restoration of the monarchy, the reaction against Puritanism was embodied in a huge output of plays, and public enthusiasm for play-going.

Restoration comedy was formed in this spirit of celebration, which was expressed not simply in the comic and satiric plots, but also in the special complicity between actor and audience. The 'shared experience' of the early converted tennis-court theatres, analogous to the atmosphere at a cabaret, or the Comedy Store today, remains as a collusive flavour throughout the plays of this fifty year period. This 'complicity' is a major key to the art of playing Restoration comedy.

The opening soliloquy of 'Sir John Brute' in Vanbrugh's *The Provoked Wife*, for example, is not so much direct address, not Sir John communing with himself, but more 'taking the ear' of the audience, sharing with people he assumes to be friends.

The second major key to these plays is the language. It is a complex, sophisticated language, playing with ideas, which the actor needs to deliver with relish and a certain intellectual energy. On a technical level, the lips and tongue need to be supple and under control, and the actor needs to think through every line just ahead of speaking. There is no Shakespearean 'music' to sustain emotion and energy.

Finally, there is such a sense of dangerous excitement, of breaking taboos in these plays. This 'edginess' comes from breaking the theatrical silence, making social and political commentary, but principally from bringing onto the stage the first English actresses, and thereby real sex. Women appeared as women in the public arena for the first time, way behind the rest of Europe. So the relationship between men and women is a central preoccupation of all these plays. What could be more modern than the 'proviso' scene in Congreve's *The Way of the World*, with the lovers, 'Mirabell' and 'Millamant', bargaining for autonomy within marriage?

Michael Attenborough

Michael Attenborough is Executive Producer with the Royal Shakespeare Company and directed *The Changeling* at The Swan in Stratford in 1992, which afterwards transferred to the Barbican, London. He also directed David Edgar's *Pentecost* at the Young Vic in 1995.

Performing a classical piece in audition presents the actor or actress with the same challenge that would face them, were they appearing in a full-scale classical production. Namely, how to do justice to and remain truthful within formal, rich poetic language. All too often a modern actor who has come across as truthful and skilled in a contemporary piece, comes a cropper with a classical speech, largely because of a failure to meet the demands of the language. This usually takes the form of attempting to pretend that a speech in poetic language is really no different from one in contemporary speech and needs only to be approached in the same way. Such intimate 'naturalistic' acting merely results in the language sounding ridiculously high flown and so, ironically,

27

the very striving to come across as real results in precisely the opposite.

The crucial challenge is to confront head-on the richness, sensuality and texture of poetic language and dramatic verse, and marry them together with psychological and emotional truth. My own conviction is that without fully exploring the former, you cannot achieve the latter.

Sadly, one all too frequently comes across emerging drama students who have not been trained sufficiently to enable them to grapple with this central challenge when confronted by a classic text. In my opinion the majority of good young actors have an appetite for language, but have not been helped to discover how to challenge such a hunger into technical terms that will enable them to immerse themselves in the language and emerge the other side with a fully realised character. If you come in 'under' the language, it merely sounds absurd; if you come in 'over the top' of the language it will sound rhetorical, grandiose and equally ridiculous. The challenge is to come in at a level of the language so that form and content seamlessly fuse together.

Obviously you need to possess a natural instinct for such work, but I firmly believe that it is often surrounded by a needless amount of mystique and fear. I have seen many actors acquire such knowledge and technique and consequently blossom and grow as performers. The best teachers and directors can help actors and actresses to achieve this. Failing that, there are some excellent guidelines laid down in invaluable books by Cicely Berry, John Barton and Patsy Rodenburg.

The challenge is not an easy one, but in my view, with work and commitment, eminently and thrillingly achievable.

Finding a good audition speech is the first step towards a successful audition.

It is interesting to see how different the speeches in this book are by comparison with modern audition pieces – so much blood, lust, incest, intrigue and murder. There is a tremendous energy and excitement about the language, and yet not a word is over-used or out of place. There is strong drama for everybody, as well as some extremely good comedy situations. But you do have to work that bit harder on preparation – particularly on **voice**, **movement** and **background of character**.

In the early seventeenth century, playwrights Thomas Heywood and John Webster especially recommended that actors paid attention to the 'art of rhetoric'. This did not necessarily mean having a 'grandiloquent' delivery, but developing the ability to communicate well and make their voices heard in a public theatre, often with a seating capacity of two to three thousand, with audiences who weren't as polite as they are today!

Movement was also considered important and dancing was held to be a great social asset. The courtiers in the reign of James I could execute the most complicated sets of steps and capers, and by the eighteenth century the aristocracy and the 'well to do' employed dancing masters, not only to teach the latest and most fashionable dances, but also to instruct their sons and daughters in 'movement and deportment'. Restoration actors such as the great Thomas Betterton and his wife, Mary Sanderson, were most meticulous about working on their characters, as indeed was Thomas Dogget, who went to such pains to perfect his 'sailor part' in *Love for Love*.

Although few of us would be prepared to go to such extremes today, we still need to do a lot more than just read the book! The New Mermaid plays, apart from giving detailed foot notes, have excellent introductions with most of the background information you need – often saving hours of searching through reference libraries. They are available at most good bookshops, but there is also a tear-out order form at the back of this book.

Auditions and preparing for auditions are part of an actor's life. It is important to keep a clear head. Find out as much as you can about the part you are auditioning for and try to find a speech from the same period or something near to it. Make sure you leave plenty of time to get there – then relax. Most people are nice and want you to succeed. And above all – enjoy yourself!

CLASSICAL
AUDITION
SPEECHES

The Alchemist

Ben Jonson

First performed at the Globe Theatre, London, by the King's Men in 1610, the action takes place in Lovewit's house in the City of London. Lovewit, having hurried away from the city to avoid the plague, has left his house in the sole charge of Jeremy, his butler. Jeremy, under the assumed name of Face, conspires with two Jacobean low life characters, Subtle, a professional alchemist and his colleague, DOL COMMON, to use his master's home to practise alchemy and other types of swindling on their rich and not so rich neighbours.

In this opening scene Face and Subtle enter quarrelling loudly, followed by DOL COMMON, who is determined to keep their noise down in case they should betray themselves and 'o'erthrow all'.

Act 1, Scene 1

DOL

                                      O me!
We are ruined! Lost! Ha' you no more regard
To your reputations? Where's your judgment? S'light,
Have yet, some care of me, o' your republic . . .
You'll bring your head within a coxcomb, will you?
[*She catcheth out Face his sword; and breaks Subtle's glass*]
And you, sir, with your menstrue, gather it up.
S'death, you abominable pair of stinkards,
Leave off your barking, and grow one again,
Or, by the light that shines, I'll cut your throats.
I'll not be made a prey unto the marshal,
For ne'er a snarling dog-bolt o' you both.
Ha' you together cozened all this while,

And all the world, and shall it now be said
You've made most courteous shift, to cozen yourselves?
[*To Face*] You will accuse him? You will bring him in
Within the statute? Who shall take your word?
A whoreson, upstart, apocryphal captain,
Whom not a puritan, in Blackfriars, will trust
So much, as for a feather! [*To Subtle*] And you, too,
Will give the cause, forsooth? You will insult,
And claim a primacy, in the divisions?
You must be chief? As if you, only, had
The powder to project with? And the work
Were not begun out of equality?
The venture tripartite? All things in common?
Without priority? 'Sdeath, you perpetual curs,
Fall to your couples again, and cozen kindly,
And heartily, and lovingly, as you should,
And lose not the beginning of a term,
Or, by this hand, I shall grow factious too,
And take my part, and quit you.

'Slight 'God's light'

republic Lat. 'common thing', i.e. Dol

You'll bring your head . . . you? you're determined to be a fool? The coxcomb was the traditional fool's headdress.

menstrue solvent

marshal provost-marshal, in charge of prisons

dog-bolt a blunt-headed arrow. Here used figuratively and with an associative logic from 'snarling'.

apocryphal fictional

powder to project with here used figuratively for criminal inventiveness

'Sdeath 'God's death'

couples the word used for a pair of hunting dogs working together

cozen kindly deceive amicably (with a pun on 'act like relatives')

term of the law courts. The four terms were periods of great business and social activity and provided opportunities for swindlers.

All for Love

John Dryden

The first recorded performance of this tragedy was at the Theatre Royal, Drury Lane, London in 1677 by the King's Company.

This is Dryden's version of the well-known love story of Mark Antony and CLEOPATRA, Queen of Egypt, with its central theme of conflict between overwhelming passion and duty to family and state, which ends in the inevitable deaths of both lovers.

Antony, having lost the battle at Actium, is persuaded by his general to leave CLEOPATRA and return to his legions in Lower Syria. In this scene CLEOPATRA begs him not to go, and when he tries to tell her that their love has only brought ruin to both of them, pleads her cause, while Antony's general, Ventidius, looks on, interrupting her speech with his caustic comments.

Act 2

CLEOPATRA
How shall I plead my cause, when you my judge,
Already have condemned me? Shall I bring
The love you bore me for my advocate?
That now is turned against me, that destroys me,
For love once past is at the best forgotten,
But oftener sours to hate: 'twill please my Lord
To ruin me, and therefore I'll be guilty.
But could I once have thought it would have pleased you,
That you would pry with narrow searching eyes
Into my faults, severe to my destruction.
And watching all advantages with care
That serve to make me wretched? Speak, my Lord,
For I end here. Though I deserve this usage,
                              ... You seem grieved
(And therein you are kind), that Caesar first
Enjoyed my love, though you deserved it better:
I grieve for that, my Lord, much more than you,
For had I first been yours, it would have saved
My second choice; I never had been his,
And ne'er had been but yours. But Caesar first,
You say, possessed my love. Not so, my Lord:
He first possessed my person, you my love;
Caesar loved me, but I loved Antony.
If I endured him after, 'twas because
I judged it due to the first name of men,
And, half constrained, I gave, as to a tyrant,
What he would take by force.

Arden of Faversham

Anon

The authorship of this tragedy remains uncertain, but it is believed to have been written sometime between 1587 and 1592. It is based on the true story of the murder of Arden, a wealthy landowner, by his young wife ALICE and her lover Mosby, some forty years earlier.

Arden has long suspected ALICE of carrying on an affair with Mosby, although the couple vehemently deny this, but has no idea of their more sinister intentions. After several attempts on Arden's life by various hired assassins, ALICE plans to meet Arden on his return from London, arm-in-arm with her lover. This will incite him to violence and she can then call on the assassins, Black Will and Shakebag, to kill him. The plan misfires and Shakebag and Mosby are both wounded. ALICE immediately turns on Arden, accusing him of drawing his sword in a needless fit of jealousy. Once more she manages to convince him that there is nothing between her and Mosby and that the arranged meeting was all in harmless 'jest'.

Scene 8

ALICE

Ah, Arden, what folly blinded thee?
Ah, jealous harebrain man what has thou done?
When we, to welcome thee, intended sport,
Came lovingly to meet thee on thy way,
Thou drew'st thy sword, enraged with jealousy,
And hurt thy friend whose thoughts were free from harm;
All for a worthless kiss and joining arms,
Both done but merrily to try thy patience.
And me unhappy that devised the jest,
Which, though begun in sport, yet ends in blood! . . .
Couldst thou not see us friendly smile on thee
When we joined arms and when I kissed his cheek?
Hast thou not lately found me over-kind?
Didst thou not hear me cry they murder thee?
Called I not help to set my husband free?
No, ears and all were 'witched. Ah me accursed,
To link in liking with a frantic man!
Henceforth I'll be thy slave, no more thy wife;
For with that name I never shall content thee.
If I be merry, thou straightways thinks me light;
If sad, thou sayest the sullens trouble me;
If well attired, thou thinks I will be gadding;
If homely, I seem sluttish in thine eye.
Thus am I still, and shall be while I die,
Poor wench abused by thy misgovernment. . . .
The heavens can witness of our harmless thoughts . . .
Nay, hadst thou loved me as thou dost pretend,
Thou wouldst have marked the speeches of thy friend,
Who going wounded from the place, he said
His skin was pierced only through my device.
And if sad sorrow taint thee for this fault
Thou wouldst have followed him and seen him dressed,
And cried him mercy whom thou hast misdone;
Ne'er shall my heart be eased till this be done.

sullens sulks
still always
while until
misdone wronged, injured

The Atheist's Tragedy

Cyril Tourneur

This is considered to be one of the last of the revenge tragedies and was most probably written in 1611. D'Amville, the atheist of the title, believes that Nature is the Supreme Force and that Man is nothing more than a superior animal, children being his only claim to immortality. Wealth is therefore of prime importance as a means of making life as pleasurable as possible, and to attain this he will stop at nothing.

CASTABELLA, daughter of Baron Belforest and heir to his fortune and estate, is betrothed to D'Amville's nephew, Charlemont. D'Amville persuades Charlemont to enlist in the army and then arranges for him to be reported dead and disinherited. CASTABELLA is then forced to marry D'Amville's son, Rousard. However, Rousard proves to be impotent and D'Amville, determined that the family line should continue, lures CASTABELLA into the churchyard late at night on the pretext of having something important to say to her.

To her horror, he declares his love for her and suggests that as his son is impotent, he himself can offer her both profit and the pleasure of his body if she will submit to him.

Act 4, Scene 3

CASTABELLA
Now Heav'n defend me! May my memory
Be utterly extinguished, and the heir
Of him that was my father's enemy
Raise his eternal monument upon
Our ruins, ere the greatest pleasure or
The greatest profit ever tempt me to
Continue it by incest . . .
O God,
Is Thy unlimited and infinite
Omnipotence less free because Thou dost
No ill? Or if you argue merely out
Of Nature, do you not degenerate
From that, and are you not unworthy the
Prerogative of Nature's masterpiece,
When basely you prescribe yourself
Authority and law from their examples
Whom you should command? I could confute
You, but the horror of the argument
Confounds my understanding. – Sir, I know
You do but try me in your son's behalf,
Suspecting that my strength and youth of blood
Cannot contain themselves with impotence.
Believe me, sir,
I never wronged him. If it be your lust,
O quench it on their prostituted flesh,
Whose trade of sin can please desire with more
Delight and less offence. – The poison of
Your breath, evaporated from so foul a soul,
Infects the air more than the damps that rise
From bodies but half rotten in their graves.

contain content
damps gases

Bartholmew Fair

Ben Jonson

This Jacobean comedy was first performed in 1614 by the Lady Elizabeth's Servants at the Hope Theatre, London. It is a lively, festive entertainment with no central hero, and no fewer than thirty-four characters, ranging from minor landed gentry to the 'common folk' who come to visit the fair, and the stall holders themselves, the entertainers, cut-purses and swindlers. This fair-ground scene is played in and around the booth of URSLA the pig-woman – roast pig being the biggest attraction of the day – and ends up at the Puppet Theatre where Littlewit's play is being performed.

   URSLA is a very large lady. Here she is seen complaining of the heat to Nightingale, the Ballad Singer, and calling to Mooncalf, her tapster, to bring her some ale, while she explains to him how to make a profit on the beer and tobacco sales.

Act 2, Scene 2

URSLA

Fie upon't! Who would wear out their youth and prime thus in roasting of pigs, that had any cooler vocation? Hell's a kind of cold cellar to't, a very fine vault, o' my conscience! What, Mooncalf! ... [*To Mooncalf*] My chair, you false faucet you; and my morning's draught, quickly, a bottle of ale to quench me, rascal. – I am all fire and fat, Nightingale, I shall e'en melt away to the first woman, a rib again, I am afraid. I do water the ground in knots as I go, like a great garden-pot; you may follow me by the S's I make ... Where's my pipe now? Not filled? Thou arrant incubee! ... How can I hope that ever he'll discharge his place of trust – tapster, a man of reckoning under me – that remembers nothing I say to him? [*Exit Nightingale*] But look to't, sirrah, you were best. Threepence a pipeful I will ha' made of all my whole half-pound of tobacco, and a quarter of a pound of coltsfoot mixed with it too, to itch it out. I that have dealt so long in the fire will not be to seek in smoke now. Then, six and twenty shillings a barrel I will advance o' my beer, and fifty shillings a hundred o' my bottle-ale; I ha' told you the ways how to raise it. Froth your cans well i' the filling at length, rogue, and jog your bottles o' the buttock, sirrah; then skink out the first glass, ever, and drink with all companies, though you be sure to be drunk; you'll misreckon the better, and be less ashamed on't. But your true trick, rascal, must be to be ever busy, and mis-take away the bottles and cans in haste before they be half drunk off, and never hear anybody call, if they should chance to mark you, till you ha' brought fresh, and be able to forswear 'em. Give me a drink of ale. ... Look who's there, sirrah! Five shillings a pig is my price – at least. If it be a sow-pig, sixpence more. If she be a great-bellied wife, and long for't, sixpence more for that.

faucet tap for a barrel
knots intricate figures of criss-cross lines
itch eke
to seek in short of
advance raise the price
at length i.e. with the can held as far below the spigot as possible
skink pour

The Beaux' Strategem

George Farquhar

First performed in 1707 at the Queen's Theatre, Haymarket, London, by Her Majesty's Sworn Comedians and set in Lichfield. The main action concerns the adventures of the two beaux, Aimwell and Archer, who travel up to Lichfield from London to recoup their 'broken fortune' and succeed in carrying off the Squire's beautiful sister Dorinda and his discontented wife, Mrs SULLEN.

In this scene, MRS SULLEN is complaining to Dorinda about life in the country and in particular, the unbearable behaviour of her drunken husband. Dorinda points out that the Squire allows her a comfortable maintenance and she shares in 'all the pleasures that the country affords'.

Act 2, Scene 1

MRS SULLEN

Country pleasures! Racks and torments! Dost think, child, that my limbs were made for leaping of ditches, and clambering over stiles? or that my parents, wisely foreseeing my future happiness in country pleasures, had early instructed me in the rural accomplishments of drinking fat ale, playing at whisk, and smoking tobacco with my husband; or of spreading of plaisters, brewing of diet-drinks, and stilling rosemary-water, with the good old gentlewoman my mother-in-law? . . . Not that I disapprove rural pleasures, as the poets have painted them; in their landscape, every Phyllis has her Corydon, every murmuring stream, and every flowery mead, gives fresh alarms to love. Besides, you'll find that their couples were never married. – But yonder I see my Corydon, and a sweet swain it is, Heaven knows! Come, Dorinda, don't be angry; he's my husband, and your brother: and, between both, is he not a sad brute? . . . O sister, sister!

If ever you marry, beware of a sullen, silent sot, one that's always musing, but never thinks. There's some diversion in a talking block-head; and since a woman must wear chains, I would have the pleasure of hearing 'em rattle a little. Now you shall see, but take this by the way: – He came home this morning at his usual hour of four, wakened me out of a sweet dream of something else, by tumbling over the tea-table, which he broke all to pieces; after his man and he had rolled about the room like sick passengers in a storm, he comes flounce into bed, dead as a salmon into a fishmonger's basket; his feet cold as ice, his breath hot as a furnace, and his hands and his face as greasy as his flannel nightcap. – O, matrimony! – He tosses up the clothes with a barbarous swing over his shoulders, disorders the whole economy of my bed, leaves me half naked, and my whole night's comfort is the tuneable serenade of that wakeful nightingale, his nose! O the pleasure of counting the melancholy clock by a snoring husband! But now, sister, you shall see how handsomely, being a well-bred man, he will beg my pardon.

fat ale strong, full-bodied ale
plaisters obsolete form of 'plasters'
diet-drinks drinks prescribed and prepared for medicinal purposes
stilling distilling
Phyllis . . . Corydon common names for a shepherdess and shepherd in pastoral poetry
swain a lover or wooer in pastoral poetry; but, also, a rustic or farm labourer, the latter meaning obviously fitting Mrs Sullen's uncomplimentary opinion of her spouse.
economy orderly arrangement
tuneable harmonious, tuneful

The Broken Heart

John Ford

Possibly published in 1633 and performed in a private house in Blackfriars, London, it is set in Sparta.

PENTHEA, in love with Orgilus, has been forced to marry Bassanes, a rich nobleman, by her ambitious brother, Ithocles. Bassanes, insanely jealous and aware of her former attachment to Orgilus, keeps her shut up at home with an old serving woman to watch over her. In this scene, Orgilus, in heavy disguise, contrives to meet PENTHEA secretly, but although she confesses that she will always love him, she is determined to abide by her marriage vows, and turns him away.

Act 2, Scene 3

PENTHEA
                                                    Remove
Your steps some distance from me: – at this space
A few words I dare change; but first put on
Your borrowed shape . . .
How, Orgilus, by promise I was thine
The Heavens do witness: they can witness too
A rape done on my truth. How I do love thee
Yet, Orgilus, and yet, must best appear
In tendering thy freedom; for I find
The constant preservation of thy merit,
By thy not daring to attempt my fame
With injury of any loose conceit,
Which might give deeper wounds to discontents.
Continue this fair race; then, though I cannot
Add to thy comfort, yet I shall more often
Remember from what fortune I am fallen,

And pity mine own ruin. Live, live happy,
Happy in thy next choice, that thou mayest people
This barren age with virtues in thy issue.
And, oh, when thou art married, think on me
With mercy, not contempt. I hope thy wife,
Hearing my story , will not scorn my fall.
Now let us part . . .
. . . Uncivil sir, forbear,
Or I can turn affection into vengeance;
Your reputation (if you value any)
Lies bleeding at my feet. Unworthy man,
If ever henceforth thou appear in language,
Message, or letter, to betray my frailty,
I'll call thy former protestations lust,
And curse my stars for forfeit of my judgement.
Go thou, fit only for disguise and walks,
To hide thy shame; this once I spare thy life.
I laugh at mine own confidence; my sorrows
By thee are made inferior to my fortunes.
If ever thou didst harbour worthy love,
Dare not to answer. My good genius guide me,
That I may never see thee more. – Go from me.

tendering cherishing
attempt my fame attack my honour
loose conceit wild idea
race course of action
for . . . judgement for misguiding me into loving you
good genius used here in the sense of 'good angel'

Bussy D'Ambois

George Chapman

This tragedy was possibly written in 1604 for the Children of the Chapel Royal, later to become the Children of the Queen's Revels.

Bussy D'Ambois is an historical figure, well known at that time for his political activities and amours at the French court of Henry III.

In the play he is likened to Hercules and sees himself as some sort of god-like avenger, striking down evil and 'cleaning out the Augean stables of the world'.* He is fiery and passionate and TAMYRA, the Count of Montsurry's wife, is immediately and fatally attracted to him, although she loves her husband dearly. In this scene TAMYRA has just said a fond goodbye to her husband who will be away on business until the next morning. She sends her maid, Pero, away and now she waits for Bussy to appear, knowing that the step she is about to take can bring nothing but ruin for both of them.

* Maurice Evans in his Introduction to the New Mermaid's edition of *Bussy D'Ambois*.

Act 2, Scene 2

TAMYRA
Farewell, my light and life. But not in him,
[In mine own dark love and light bent to another.]
Alas, that in the wane of our affections
We should supply it with a full dissembling,
In which each youngest maid is grown a mother.
Frailty is fruitful, one sin gets another:
Our loves like sparkles are, that brightest shine
When they go out; most vice shows most divine.
– Go maid, to bed; lend me your book, I pray:
Not, like yourself, for form; I'll this night trouble
None of your services: make sure the doors,
And call your other fellows to their rest. . . .
Now all the peaceful regents of the night,
Silently-gliding exhalations,
Languishing winds, and murmuring falls of waters,
Sadness of heart and ominous secureness,
Enchantments, dead sleeps, all the friends of rest,
That ever wrought upon the life of man,
Extend your utmost strengths, and this charmed hour
Fix like the Centre! Make the violent wheels
Of Time and Fortune stand, and great Existence,
the Maker's treasury, now not seem to be,
To all but my approaching friends and me!
They come, alas, they come! Fear, fear and hope
Of one thing, at one instant, fight in me:
I love what most I loathe, and cannot live,
Unless I compass that which holds my death:
For love is hateful without love again,
And he I love, will loathe me, when he sees
I fly my sex, my virtue, my renown,
To run so madly on a man unknown. [*The vault opens.*]
See, see, the gulf is opening that will swallow
Me and my fame for ever; I will in,
and cast myself off, as I ne'er had been.

sparkles sparks
regents rulers

The Changeling

Thomas Middleton & William Rowley

First produced in 1622 at the Phoenix Theatre, Drury Lane, London, and performed by the Lady Elizabeth's Players, it is set in Alicante on the east coast of Spain.

At the beginning of the play, BEATRICE JOANNA, betrothed to Alonzo De Piracquo, falls deeply in love with the nobleman, Alsemero. In desperation she hires her father's servant De Flores, a man she finds physically repulsive, to kill Alonzo. De Flores has lusted long and secretly after BEATRICE and kills Alonzo in order to gain power over her. When he comes to claim his reward he refuses the money she offers and insists that she surrenders her body to him instead, otherwise he will divulge her part in the murder. In this scene she has just married Alsemero, having already been forced to submit to De Flores. She is dreading her wedding night. In her husband's closet she finds strange potions and recipes to test for virginity and signs of pregnancy.

Act 4, Scene 1

BEATRICE
This fellow has undone me endlessly:
Never was bride so fearfully distressed.
The more I think upon th'ensuing night,
And whom I am to cope with in embraces –
One who's ennobled both in blood and mind,
So clear in understanding (that's my plague now),
Before whose judgement will my fault appear
Like malefactors' crimes before tribunals
(There is no hiding on't) – the more I dive
Into my own distress. How a wise man
Stands for a great calamity! There's no venturing

Into his bed, what course soe'er I light upon,
Without my shame, which may grow up to danger.
He cannot but in justice strangle me
As I lie by him, as a cheater use me;
'Tis a precious craft to play with a false die
Before a cunning gamester. Here's his closet,
The key left in't, and he abroad i' th' park;
Sure 'twas forgot, I'll be so bold as look in't.

                                        [*Opens closet*]

Bless me! A right physician's closet 'tis,
Set round with vials, every one her mark too . . .
'How to know whether a woman be a maid or not.'
If that should be applied, what would become of me?
Belike he has a strong faith of my purity,
That never yet made proof; but this he calls
'A merry sleight, but true experiment, the author
Antonius Mizaldus. Give the party you suspect the quan-
tity of a spoonful of the water in the glass M, which upon
her that is a maid makes three several effects: 'twill make
her incontinently gape, then fall into a sudden sneezing,
last into a violent laughing; else dull, heavy, and lumpish.'
Where had I been?
I fear it, yet 'tis seven hours to bedtime.

---

fellow 'man of lower rank and no worth'; also and ironically = 'accomplice' and 'husband'
undone (1) ruined; (2) had intercourse with. Also perhaps = 'deprived of copulation' (i.e. ironically, with Alsemero).
endlessly no doubt used more loosely by Beatrice than by M
distressed also = sexually deprived – which as a *bride*, she will be
Stands for represents, or stands open to
use (also) copulate with
precious i.e. obtainable only at great cost – so 'risky' and/or 'difficult'
die singular of 'dice'
closet small private room – located within the inner stage
right true, veritable
vials small containers holding liquid medicine
Belike . . . proof perhaps, not having tested my purity, he has strong faith in it and will there-fore not proceed to do so (ironic in several ways)
sleight trick
several different
incontinently immediately
else further

The Country Wife

William Wycherley

First performed in 1675, probably at the Theatre Royal, Drury Lane, London by the King's Company. Jack Pinchwife, an old rake, has married a pretty young country girl and is determined to keep her away from the young 'gallants' about town. When he discovers that the notorious Master Horner has been paying his attentions to her and has even kissed her, he orders his young wife to sit down and write a letter to Master Horner telling him how much she hates and detests him. However, when he goes off to fetch wax and candle to seal it, MRS PINCHWIFE determines to write a second letter and exchange it for the first.

Act 4, Scene 2

MRS PINCHWIFE

'For Master Horner' – So, I am glad he has told me his name. Dear Master Horner! But why should I send thee such a letter that will vex thee and make thee angry with me? – Well, I will not send it. – Ay, but then my husband will kill me – for I see plainly, he won't let me love Master Horner – but what care I for my husband? – I won't, so I won't send poor Master Horner such a letter – but then my husband – But oh, what if I writ at bottom, my husband made me write it? – Ay, but then my husband would see't – Can one have no shift? Ah, a London woman would have had a hundred presently. Stay – what if I should write a letter, and wrap it up like this, and write upon't too? Ay, but then my husband would see't – I don't know what to do – But yet i'vads I'll try, so I will – for I will not send this letter to poor Master Horner, come what will on't.
[*She writes, and repeats what she hath writ*]
'Dear Sweet Master Horner' – so – 'My husband would have me send you a base, rude, unmannerly letter – but I won't' – so – 'and would have me forbid you loving me – but I won't' – so – 'and would have me say to you, I hate you poor Master Horner – but I won't tell a lie for him' – there – 'for I'm sure if you and I were in the country at cards together' – so – 'I could not help treading on your toe under the table' – so – 'or rubbing knees with you, and staring in your face till you saw me' – very well – 'and then looking down and blushing for an hour together' – so – 'but I must make haste before my husband come; and now he has taught me to write letters, you shall have longer ones from me, who am, dear, dear, poor dear Master Horner, your most humble friend, and servant to command till death, Margery Pinchwife'. – Stay, I must give him a hint at bottom – so – now wrap it up just like t'other – so now write 'For Master Horner'. – But, oh now, what shall I do with it? For here comes my husband.

shift expedient
i'vads in faith; rustic oath
hint at bottom i.e. the postcript read by Horner at Act 4, sc. 3 286–9

The Critic

Richard Brinsley Sheridan

First performed at Drury Lane in 1799, this comedy of manners is set in London and satirises plays of romantic love and patriotic excess.

In the opening scene, MRS DANGLE, the nagging wife of a theatre critic, is sitting at breakfast with her husband while he reads the newspapers aloud to her. He is only concerned with the latest theatrical gossip, while she prefers to hear about the current political crisis. She is unimpressed when he announces that his friend, Mr Puff, has written a new tragedy to be performed at the Drury Lane Theatre.

Act 1, Scene 1

MRS DANGLE

Lord, Mr Dangle, why will you plague me about such nonsense? – Now the plays are begun I shall have no peace. – Isn't it sufficient to make yourself ridiculous by your passion for the theatre, without continually teasing me to join you? Why can't you ride your hobby-horse without desiring to place me on a pillion behind you, Mr Dangle? ... No, no; you never will read anything that's worth listening to:– you hate to hear about your country; there are letters every day with Roman signatures, demonstrating the certainty of an invasion, and proving that the nation is utterly undone – But you never will read anything to entertain one ... And what have you to do with the theatre, Mr Dangle? Why should you affect the character of a Critic? I have no patience with you! – haven't you made yourself the jest of all your acquaintance by your interference in matters where you have no business? Are not you called a theatrical Quidnunc, and a mock Maecenas to second-hand authors?... Yes, truly; you have contrived to get a share in all the plague and trouble of theatrical property, without the profit, or even the credit of the abuse that attends it ... And to be sure it is extremely pleasant to have one's house made the motley rendezvous of all the lackeys of literature! – The very high change of trading authors and jobbing critics! – Yes, my drawing room is an absolute register office for candidate actors, and poets without character; – then to be continually alarmed with Misses and Ma'ams piping hysteric changes on JULIETS and DORINDAS, POLLYS and OPHELIAS; and the very furniture trembling at the probationary starts and unprovoked rants of would-be RICHARDS and HAMLETS! – And what is worse than all, now that the Manager has monopolized the Opera House, haven't we the Signors and Signioras calling here, sliding their smooth semibreves, and gargling glib divisions in their outlandish throats – with foreign emissaries and French spies, for aught I know, disguised like fiddlers and figure dancers! ... And to employ yourself so idly at such an alarming crisis as this too – when, if you had the least spirit, you would have been at the head of one of the Westminster associations – or trailing a volunteer pike in the Artillery Ground! – But you – o' my conscience, I believe if the French were landed tomorrow, your first enquiry would be, whether they had brought a theatrical troupe with them.

entertain Mrs Dangle's concern seems not itself very agonised.

character of a Critic Bayes, a character in *The Rehearsal*, loathes critics: 'there are, now-a-days, a sort of persons, they call Critiques, that, I gad, have no more wit in them than so many Hobby-horses; but they'll laugh you, Sir, and find fault, and censure things' (*The Rehearsal* I.i.307–10). Sheridan's spelling of the word 'critic' without the final 'k' occasioned comment. The story was told in the *Morning Chronicle* of 15 December 1779 that Sheridan meant to intimate by this short spelling on the play bills 'that the Piece was not *finished* when the bills were printed'.

Quidnunc from *quid nunc?* what now? – a newsmonger, a gossip

Maecenas the patron of Virgil and Horace, and so a name for any literary patron

second-hand unoriginal

The Double-Dealer

William Congreve

This Restoration comedy was first performed in 1693 at the Theatre Royal, London, by Their Majesties' Servants and is set in Lord Touchwood's House on the eve of the wedding of his nephew, Mellefont, and Sir Paul Plyant's daughter, Cynthia. The main action centres on the plot against Mellefont by his 'double dealing friend' Maskwell, who is himself in love with Cynthia, and is determined the marriage will not take place. He enlists the help of the dangerous Lady Touchwood, who persuades LADY PLYANT, Sir Paul's foolish wife, that Mellefont is in love with her, knowing that she in turn will tell Sir Paul who will put an immediate stop to the wedding. In this scene, LADY PLYANT accuses the bewildered Mellefont of wishing to seduce her, and when he falls to his knees pleading that he meant no such thing, takes this as yet another proof of his passion.

Act 2, Scene 2

LADY PLYANT

Oh name it no more – bless me, how can you talk of heaven, and
have so much wickedness in your heart? Maybe you don't think it a
sin, – they say some of you gentlemen don't think it a sin, – maybe
it is no sin to them that don't think it so; – indeed, if I did not think
it a sin, – but still my honour, if it were no sin, – but then, to marry
my daughter, for the conveniency of frequent opportunities, – I'll
never consent to that, as sure as can be, I'll break the match . . . Nay,
nay, rise up, come you shall see my good nature. [*He rises*] I know
love is powerful, and nobody can help his passion: 'tis not your fault;
nor I swear it is not mine. – How can I help it, if I have charms? And
how can you help it, if you are made a captive; I swear it's pity it
should be a fault, – but my honour – well, but your honour too – but
the sin! – Well but the necessity – oh Lord, here's somebody coming,
I dare not stay. Well, you must consider of your crime; and strive as
much as can be against it, – strive be sure – but don't be melancholy,
don't despair, – but never think that I'll grant you anything; oh Lord,
no; – but be sure you lay aside all thoughts of the marriage, for
though I know you don't love Cynthia, only as a blind for your passion to me; yet it will make me jealous, – oh Lord, what did I say?
Jealous! No, no, I can't be jealous, for I must not love you, – therefore don't hope, – but don't despair neither, – oh, they're coming, I
must fly.

The Duchess of Malfi

John Webster

The first performance by the King's Men was most probably sometime between 1612 and 1614, being presented privately at Blackfriars and publicly at the Globe Theatre in London. It is set in Malfi and in Rome and concerns the tragedy that follows the liaison and subsequent marriage of the widowed DUCHESS OF MALFI and her steward Antonio, and the jealousy of her two brothers – one the Cardinal and the other her twin, Ferdinand, who hire the devilish Bosola to spy on her and eventually murder her. In this scene the DUCHESS is imprisoned with her waiting-woman, Cariola and her two children. They have been tormented by madmen brought in from the local hospital and now Bosola enters disguised as an old man with a cord in his hands. The DUCHESS is to be strangled. She calls to Cariola to look after her children, and then addressing Bosola, prepares herself for death.

Act 4, Scene 2

[*Executioners seize Cariola, who struggles*]
DUCHESS

                                    Farewell Cariola,
In my last will I have not much to give;
A many hungry guests have fed upon me,
Thine will be a poor reversion . . .
I pray thee look thou giv'st my little boy
Some syrup for his cold, and let the girl
Say her prayers, ere she sleep. [*Cariola is forced off*]
                              Now what you please,
What death? . . . Not a whit:
What would it pleasure me, to have my throat cut
With diamonds? or to be smothered
With cassia? or to be shot to death, with pearls?
I know death hath ten thousand several doors
. For men to take their *Exits*: and 'tis found
They go on such strange geometrical hinges,
You may open them both ways: any way, for Heaven sake,
So I were out of your whispering. Tell my brothers
That I perceive death, now I am well awake,
Best gift is, they can give, or I can take.
I would fain put off my last woman's fault,
I'll'd not be tedious to you. . .
Dispose my breath how please you, but my body
Bestow upon my women, will you? . . .
Pull, and pull strongly, for your able strength
Must pull down heaven upon me:
Yet stay, heaven gates are not so highly arch'd
As princes' palaces: they that enter there
Must go upon their knees. [*Kneels*] Come violent death,
Serve for mandragora to make me sleep;
Go tell my brothers, when I am laid out,
They then may feed in quiet.
                              [*They strangle her.*]

reversion something inherited upon the death of the holder
mandragora mandrake plant, taken by Webster's contemporaries to be a kind of narcotic

Eastward Ho!

Ben Jonson, George Chapman & John Marston

This Jacobean 'city comedy' seems to have been first performed in 1605 at Blackfriars, London by the Children of Her Majestie's Revels, and is the result of the successful collaboration of three well-known and respected playwrights. 'Eastward Ho!' was the cry of the Thames boatmen to hail passengers down the river to Greenwich, that is towards the Court and the prospect of adventure and 'easy gold'. The action centres around Touchstone, a Goldsmith whose belief in the older order of society where hard work, thrift and honesty win out in the end, is treated with scorn by his wife and eldest daughter, the haughty GERTRUDE.

In this scene, GERTRUDE is talking to her sister, Mildred, while she awaits the arrival of her suitor, Sir Petronel Flash, a new-made knight.

Act 1, Scene 2

GERTRUDE

For the passion of patience, look if Sir Petronel approach; that sweet, that fine, that delicate, that – for love's sake, tell me if he come. O sister Mill, though my father be a low-capped tradesman, yet I must be a lady; and, I praise God, my mother must call me Madam. (Does he come?) Off with this gown for shame's sake, off with this gown! Let not my knight take me in the city-cut in any hand. Tear't, pax on't – does he come? – tear't off! [*Sings*] *Thus whilst she sleeps, I sorrow for her sake, etc.*. . . . I tell you I cannot endure it, I must be a lady: do you wear your coif with a London licket, your stammel petticoat with two guards, the buffin gown with the tuf-taffety cape, and the velvet lace. I must be a lady, and I will be a lady. I like some humours of the city dames well: to eat cherries only at an angel a pound, good. To dye rich scarlet black, pretty. To line a grogram gown clean through with velvet, tolerable. Their pure linen, their smocks of three pound a smock, are to be borne withal. But your mincing niceries, taffeta pipkins, durance petticoats, and silver bodkins – God's my life, as I shall be a lady, I cannot endure it! Is he come yet? Lord, what a long knight 'tis! [*Sings*] *And ever she cried, Shoot home!* – and yet I knew one longer – *And ever she cried, Shoot home! Fa, la ly, re, lo, la!* . . . Alas! Poor Mill, when I am a lady, I'll pray for thee yet, i'faith: nay, and I'll vouchsafe to call thee Sister Mill still; for though thou art not like to be a lady as I am, yet sure thou art a creature of God's making, and mayest peradventure to be saved as soon as I – does he come? [*Sings, and monkey cartwheels*] . . . Is my knight come? O the Lord, my band? Sister, do my cheeks look well? Give me a little box o' the ear that I may seem to blush; now, now. So, there, there, there! Here he is! O my dearest delight! Lord, Lord, and how does my knight?

---

in any hand in any case
smock woman's undergarment
pipkins hats
durance a stout durable cloth
And ever she cried etc. An unidentified ballad with markedly sexual overtones.

Edward the Second

Christopher Marlowe

First performed possibly in the last few months of 1592 by the Earl of Pembroke's Company and published shortly after Marlowe's death.

Edward the Second is a weak and foolish king, whose infatuation for the courtier, Pierce de Gaveston, angers the barons and brings about his eventual downfall and horrifying death.

Gaveston, banished from the kingdom by Edward's father, has been living in exile in France. Now the old King is dead and Edward has summoned back his 'favourite' to share his kingdom with him. QUEEN ISABELLA, daughter of the King of France, has good reason to dislike Gaveston, and when the barons demand that he be sent away again, Edward accuses her of being instrumental in their decision. He calls her a French strumpet and tells her 'not to come within his sight' until Gaveston 'be repealed'.

Act 1, Scene 4

QUEEN
Oh miserable and distressed queen!
Would when I left sweet France and was embarked,
That charming Circe walking on the waves,
Had changed my shape, or at the marriage day
The cup of Hymen had been full of poison,
Or with those arms that twined about my neck,
I had been stifled, and not lived to see
The king my lord thus to abandon me;
Like frantic Juno will I fill the earth
With ghastly murmur of my sighs and cries,
For never doted Jove on Ganymede
So much as he on cursed Gaveston;
But that will more exasperate his wrath;
I must entreat him, I must speak him fair,
And be a means to call home Gaveston;
And yet he'll ever dote on Gaveston,
And so am I for ever miserable.

Epicoene *or* The Silent Woman

Ben Jonson

First performed by the Children of Her Majestie's Revels, most probably in 1609 and described in Jonson's own words as 'a comedy of affliction'. Most of the characters are 'epicene' in some way or other, and the Silent Woman of the title herself turns out to be a man by the end of the play.

The action centres around Morose, an elderly man obsessed with the need for absolute silence, who decides to marry only because he wishes to disinherit his nephew, and has even gone to the extent of employing someone to find him a dumb woman, whose silence will be 'dowry enough'. MISTRESS OTTER, wife of Captain Otter the bear keeper is an example of what Morose dreads most in a woman. Described as an 'Amazonian china-woman' she has been known to beat her husband into submission.

In this scene we meet her for the first time – scolding Captain Otter for his incivility among 'great ladies' and threatening to cut his allowance.

Act 3, Scene 1

MISTRESS OTTER

By that light, I'll ha' you chained up with your bull-dogs and bear-dogs, if you be not civil the sooner. I'll send you to kennel, i'faith. You were best bait me with your bull, bear, and horse! Never a time that the courtiers or collegiates come to the house, but you make it a Shrove Tuesday! I would have you get your Whitsuntide velvet cap and your staff i' your hand to entertain 'em; yes, in troth, do. . . . 'Fore me, I will 'na-ture' 'em over to Paris Garden and 'na-ture' you thither too, if you pronounce 'em again. Is a bear a fit beast, or a bull, to mix in society with great ladies? Think i' your discretion, in any good polity? . . . By my integrity, I'll send you over to the Bankside, I'll commit you to the master of the Garden, if I hear but a syllable more. Must my house, or my roof, be polluted with the scent of bears and bulls, when it is perfumed for great ladies? Is this according to the instrument when I married you? That I would be princess and reign in mine own house, and you would be my subject and obey me? What did you bring me, should make you thus peremptory? Do I allow you your half-crown a day to spend where you will among your gamesters, to vex and torment me at such times as these? Who gives you your maintenance, I pray you? Who allows you your horse-meat and man's meat? Your three suits of apparel a year? Your four pair of stockings, one silk, three worsted? Your clean linen, your bands and cuffs, when I can get you to wear 'em? 'Tis mar'l you ha' 'em on now. Who graces you with courtiers or great personages, to speak to you out of their coaches, and come home to your house? Were you ever so much as looked upon by a lord, or a lady, before I married you, but on the Easter or Whitsun holidays, and then out at the Banqueting House window, when Ned Whiting or George Stone were at the stake? . . . Answer me to that. And did not I take you up from thence in an old greasy buff-doublet, with points, and green vellet sleeves out at the elbows? You forget this . . . Oh, here are some o' the gallants! Go to, behave yourself distinctly, and with good morality, or I protest, I'll take away your exhibition.

were best had best
with along with
'Fore me before me, a common asseveration
discretion judgement
good polity affectedly for 'well-run community'
instrument formal legal agreement
horse-meat horse-fodder
hands collars
mar'l marvel
buff-doublet leather jerkin, as worn by common soldiers
points laces
vellet velvet
exhibition allowance

A Fair Quarrel

Thomas Middleton & William Rowley

This tragi-comedy set in London was most probably written in 1614 and performed by The Prince's Servants. The main action concerns the quarrel between Captain Ager and the Colonel, which continues to flare up throughout the play, always with a new 'point of honour' at stake, until the inevitable duel is fought, the Colonel is wounded and there is a final reconciliation.

Early in the action the Colonel calls Captain Ager a 'son of a whore' and the Captain swears to avenge this insult to both his mother and himself. His mother, LADY AGER, in order to avoid bloodshed, pretends to her son that she was unfaithful to his father and therefore there is nothing to fight about. However, the Captain's friends insist that he must honour his vow.

In this scene, LADY AGER asks the whereabouts of her son, and is told reluctantly by her servants that he has gone to 'meet' the Colonel.

Act 3, Scene 3

LADY AGER
                              Oh, he's lost, he's gone!
For all my pains, he's gone! Two meeting torrents
Are not so merciless as their two rages:
He never comes again. – Wretched affection!
Have I belied my faith? injured my goodness?
Slandered my honour for his preservation,
Having but only him, and yet no happier?
'Tis then a judgement plain: truth's angry with me,
In that I would abuse her sacred whiteness
For any worldly temporal respect.
Forgive me then, thou glorious woman's virtue,
Admired wher'er thy habitation is,
Especially in us weak ones; oh, forgive me,
For 'tis thy vengeance this. To belie truth,
Which is so hardly ours, with such pain purchased,
Fastings and prayers, continence and care,
Misery must needs ensue. Let him not die
In that unchaste belief of his false birth
And my disgrace; whatever angel guides him,
May this request be with my tears obtained,
Let his soul know my honour is unstained. –
Run, seek, away! If there be any hope, [Exeunt Servants]
Let me not lose him yet. When I think on him,
His dearness and his worth, it earns me more:
They that know riches tremble to be poor.
My passion is not every woman's sorrow:
She must be truly honest feels my grief,
And only known to one; if such there be,
They know the sorrow that oppresseth me. [Exit]

affection love
whiteness purity
thou ... virtue chastity
Which ... ours which we attain with so much difficulty
it ... more I am the more afflicted by grief
passion (i) suffering (ii) passionate feeling

An Ideal Husband

Oscar Wilde

This society comedy was first performed in 1895 at the Haymarket Theatre, London. The opening scene is set in the Grosvenor Square home of Sir Robert Chiltern, respected politician and Under Secretary for Foreign Affairs. He and his wife are entertaining guests in the Octagon room when Lady Markby arrives, accompanied by the fascinating but unscrupulous MRS CHEVELEY. During the evening MRS CHEVELEY contrives to speak with Sir Robert privately. She has a very large investment in the Argentine Canal scheme, which Sir Robert has denounced as a 'commonplace Stock Exchange swindle'. She informs him that it will be in his interests to reconsider this opinion and withdraw the report that he had intended to lay before the House the following night. If he refuses to do this she has information in her possession that will ruin him.

Act 1

MRS CHEVELEY

My dear Sir Robert, what then? You are ruined, that is all! Remember to what a point your Puritanism in England has brought you. In old days nobody pretended to be a bit better than his neighbours. In fact, to be a bit better than one's neighbour was considered excessively vulgar and middle-class. Nowadays, with our modern mania for morality, everyone has to pose as a paragon of purity, incorruptibility, and all the other seven deadly virtues – and what is the result? You all go over like ninepins – one after the other. Not a year passes in England without somebody disappearing. Scandals used to lend charm, or at least interest, to a man – now they crush him. And yours is a very nasty scandal. You couldn't survive it. If it were known that as a young man, secretary to a great and important minister, you sold a Cabinet secret for a large sum of money, and that that was the origin of your wealth and career, you would be hounded out of public life, you would disappear completely. And after all, Sir Robert, why should you sacrifice your entire future rather than deal diplomatically with your enemy? For the moment I am your enemy. I admit it! And I am much stronger than you are. The big battalions are on my side. You have a splendid position, but it is your splendid position that makes you so vulnerable. You can't defend it! And I am in attack. Of course I have not talked morality to you. You must admit in fairness that I have spared you that. Years ago you did a clever, unscrupulous thing; it turned out a great success. You owe to it your fortune and position. And now you have got to pay for it. Sooner or later we all have to pay for what we do. You have to pay now. Before I leave you tonight, you have got to promise me to suppress your report, and to speak in the House in favour of this scheme . . . I will be in the Ladies' Gallery tomorrow night at half-past eleven. If by that time – and you will have had heaps of opportunity – you have made an announcement to the House in the terms I wish, I shall hand you back your letter with the prettiest thanks, and the best, or at any rate the most suitable compliment I can think of. I intend to play quite fairly with you. One should always play fairly . . . when one has the winning cards. The Baron taught me that . . . amongst other things.

The Importance of Being Earnest

Oscar Wilde

This comedy of manners was first performed at the St James's Theatre, London in 1895. LADY BRACKNELL has arrived for tea at her nephew Algernon's flat in Half Moon Street, accompanied by her daughter Gwendolen. She is expecting Algernon to dine with them that evening, but he makes the excuse that he has just had a telegram saying that his poor friend, Bunbury, has been taken ill again and he must go to him at once.

Act 1

LADY BRACKNELL

It is very strange. This Mr Bunbury seems to suffer from curiously bad health . . . Well, I must say, Algernon, that I think it is high time that Mr Bunbury made up his mind whether he was going to live or to die. This shilly-shallying with the question is absurd. Nor do I in any way approve of the modern sympathy with invalids. I consider it morbid. Illness of any kind is hardly a thing to be encouraged in others. Health is the primary duty of life. I am always telling that to your poor uncle, but he never seems to take much notice – as far as any improvement in his ailments goes. I should be much obliged if you would ask Mr Bunbury, from me, to be kind enough not to have a relapse on Saturday, for I rely on you to arrange my music for me. It is my last reception, and one wants something that will encourage conversation, particularly at the end of the season when everyone has practically said whatever they had to say, which, in most cases, was probably not much . . . [*Rising and following Algernon*] I'm sure the programme will be delightful, after a few expurgations. French songs I cannot possibly allow. People always seem to think that they are improper, and either look shocked, which is vulgar, or laugh, which is worse. But German sounds a thoroughly respectable language, and indeed, I believe is so. Gwendolen, you will accompany me.

The Importance of Being Earnest

Oscar Wilde

This comedy of manners was first performed in 1895 at the St James's Theatre, London. GWENDOLEN, only daughter of Lord and Lady Bracknell, has just become engaged to Jack Worthing – known at the beginning of the play as 'Ernest'. However, when Lady Bracknell finds that 'Ernest' has 'lost' both his parents and was found in a hand-bag at Victoria Station, she forbids the match unless he can produce at least one parent by the end of the season. 'Ernest' has been telling his friend Algernon the bad news, when GWENDOLEN enters. She asks Algernon to turn his back while she has a word with 'Ernest' in private.

Act 1

GWENDOLEN

Algy, kindly turn your back. I have something very particular to say to Mr Worthing ... Ernest, we may never be married. From the expression on mamma's face I fear we never shall. Few parents nowadays pay any regard to what their children say to them. The old-fashioned respect for the young is fast dying out. Whatever influence I ever had over mamma, I lost at the age of three. But although she may prevent us from becoming man and wife, and I may marry someone else, and marry often, nothing that she can possibly do can alter my eternal devotion to you ... The story of your romantic origin, as related to me by mamma, with unpleasing comments, has naturally stirred the deeper fibres of my nature. Your Christian name has an irresistible fascination. The simplicity of your character makes you exquisitely incomprehensible to me. Your town address at the Albany I have. What is your address in the country? ... There is a good postal service, I suppose? It may be necessary to do something desperate. That of course will require serious consideration. I will communicate with you daily. ... How long do you remain in town? ... Algy, you may turn round now.

The Knight of the Burning Pestle

Francis Beaumont

First performed sometime in 1610 or 1611 at the Blackfriars Theatre, London and set in London, it is a play within a play and a satire of the merchant class with their taste for knight-errants and damsels in distress. A grocer takes his wife to see *The London Merchant* – a play about the contest for the hand of the Merchant's daughter, LUCE, between the 'gentle', but stupid Humphrey and the 'prodigal' apprentice Jasper. Throughout the performance the grocer and his wife insist on directing the action, to suit their own particular fancies, even to the extent of going up onto the stage and demanding that their boy 'Rafe' is given a main part. In this scene Jasper, pretending to be dead, has his body carried into the merchant's house and up to the room where LUCE has been locked away until she can be married to Humphrey. The boy bearing the coffin tells LUCE that before he died, Jasper commanded that his body should be brought to her 'to crave a tear from those fair eyes'.

Act 4

LUCE
Good friends, depart a little, whilst I take
My leave of this dead man that once I lov'd:
                    [*Exeunt Coffin Carrier and Boy*]
Hold yet a little, life, and then I give thee
To thy first heavenly being. Oh, my friend!
Hast thou deceived me thus, and got before me?
I shall not long be after. But, believe me,
Thou wert too cruel, Jasper, 'gainst thyself
In punishing the fault I could have pardoned,
With so untimely death. Thou didst not wrong me,

72

But ever were most kind, most true, most loving;
And I the most unkind, most false, most cruel.
Didst thou but ask a tear? I'll give thee all,
Even all my eyes can pour down, all my sighs,
And all myself, before thou goest from me.
These are but sparing rites; but if thy soul
Be yet about this place, and can behold
And see what I prepare to deck thee with,
It shall go up, borne on the wings of peace,
And satisfied. First will I sing thy dirge,
Then kiss thy pale lips, and then die myself,
And fill one coffin and one grave together.

SONG

Come you whose loves are dead,
And whiles I sing
Weep and wring
Every hand, and every head
Bind with cypress and sad yew;
Ribands black and candles blue
For him that was of men most true.
Come with heavy moaning,
And on his grave
Let him have
Sacrifice of sighs and groaning;
Let him have fair flowers enow,
White and purple, green and yellow.
For him that was of most men true.

Thou sable cloth, sad cover of my joys,
I lift thee up, and thus I meet with death.
[*Jasper rising out of the coffin*] . . .
                              . . . Save me, heaven!

Lady Windermere's Fan

Oscar Wilde

This society comedy or comedy of manners, was first performed at the St James's Theatre, London, in 1892 and is set in fashionable London. Lady Windermere, disturbed by rumours that her husband is having an affair with the notorious divorcee, MRS ERLYNNE, and finding out that he has been paying her large sums of money, decides to run away with Lord Darlington. MRS ERLYNNE, who unknown to Lady Windermere is her own mother, but has been paid by Lord Windermere to keep silent about the relationship, discovers the 'farewell note'. She hurries over to Lord Darlington's rooms, determined to prevent her daughter making the same mistake that she herself made so many years ago.

Act 3

MRS ERLYNNE

[*Starts, with a gesture of pain. Then restrains herself, and comes over to where Lady Windemere is sitting. As she speaks, she stretches out her hands towards her, but does not dare to touch her.*]

Believe what you choose about me. I am not worth a moment's sorrow. But don't spoil your beautiful young life on my account! You don't know what may be in store for you, unless you leave this house at once. You don't know what it is to fall into the pit, to be despised, mocked, abandoned, sneered at – to be an outcast! to find the door shut against one, to have to creep in by hideous byways, afraid every moment lest the mask should be stripped from one's face, and all the while to hear the laughter, the horrible laughter of the world, a thing more tragic than all the tears the world has ever shed. You don't know what it is. One pays for one's sin, and then one pays again, and all one's life one pays. You must never know that. – As for me, if suffering be an expiation, then at this moment I have expiated all my faults, whatever they have been; for tonight you have made a heart in one who had it not, made it and broken it. – But let that pass. I may have wrecked my own life, but I will not let you wreck yours. You – why, you are a mere girl, you would be lost. You haven't got the kind of brains that enables a woman to get back. You have neither the wit nor the courage. You couldn't stand dishonour. No! Go back, Lady Windermere, to the husband who loves you, whom you love. You have a child, Lady Windermere. Go back to that child who even now, in pain or in joy, may be calling to you. [*Lady Windermere rises*] God gave you that child. He will require from you that you make his life fine, that you watch over him. What answer will you make to God if his life is ruined through you? Back to your house, Lady Windermere – your husband loves you! He has never swerved for a moment from the love he bears you. But even if he had a thousand loves, you must stay with your child. If he was harsh to you, you must stay with your child. If he ill-treated you, you must stay with your child. If he abandoned you, your place is with your child . . .

[*Is about to embrace her. Then restrains herself. There is a look of wonderful joy in her face.*] Come! Where is your cloak? [*Getting it from the sofa.*] Here. Put it on. Come at once!

Love for Love

William Congreve

This Restoration comedy was first performed in 1695 by His Majesty's Servants in a theatre in Lincoln's Inn Fields, London and is set in London. ANGELICA is a young woman with a mind and a fortune of her own, living with her uncle, old Foresight. He is an illiterate and superstitious fellow, who pretends to understand astrology, dreams and omens, which rule his whole life.

In this scene he is talking to his daughter's nurse as he prepares to leave for a meeting with Sir Sampson Legend. ANGELICA comes in to ask if she may borrow his coach and he refuses. His wife and daughter have already gone out and he refers his niece to an old Arabian prophecy whereby if a man leaves his house he must make sure a woman stays at home lest he be 'cuckolded'. ANGELICA laughs at this nonsense, threatening to indict him as a wizard if she can't get her own way, and even going as far as to expose the black magic rituals he indulges in with his daughter's nurse.

Act 2, Scene 3

ANGELICA

Is not it a good hour for pleasure, too? Uncle, pray lend me your coach; mine's out of order ... I can neither make you a cuckold, uncle, by going abroad; nor secure you from being one, by staying at home ... I have a mind to go abroad; and if you won't lend me your coach, I'll take a hackney or a chair and leave you to erect a scheme and find who's in conjunction with your wife. Why don't you keep her at home, if you're jealous when she's abroad? You know my aunt is a little retrograde (as you call it) in her nature. Uncle, I'm afraid you are not lord of the ascendant, ha, ha, ha! ... Nay, uncle, don't be angry. If you are, I'll reap up all your false prophecies, ridiculous dreams and idle divinations. I'll swear you are a nuisance to the neighbourhood. What a bustle did you keep against the last invisible eclipse, laying in provision, as 'twere for a siege? What a world of fire and candle, matches and tinderboxes did you purchase! One would have thought we were ever after to live underground, or at least making a voyage to Greenland to inhabit there all the dark season ... Will you lend me your coach, or I'll go on – nay, I'll declare how your prophesied Popery was coming, only because the butler had mislaid some of the apostle's spoons and thought they were lost. Away went religion and spoon-meat together. Indeed, uncle, I'll indict you for a wizard ... Yes, I can make oath of your unlawful midnight practices; you and the old nurse there – ... Yes, I saw you together, through the keyhole of the closet, one night, like Saul and the Witch of Endor, turning the sieve and shears, and pricking your thumbs, to write poor innocent servants' names in blood, about a little nutmeg-grater, which she had forgot in the caudle-cup. Nay, I know something worse, if I would speak of it – ... I care not, but all shall out then. – Look to it, nurse; I can bring witness that you have a great unnatural teat under your left arm, and he another; and that you suckle a young devil in the shape of a tabby-cat by turns; I can.

erect a scheme calculate by astrology
spoon-meat broth, soft food given to infants
caudle-cup 'thin gruel, mixed with wine or ale, sweetened and spiced'

The Malcontent

John Marston

This tragi-comedy seems to have been written sometime between 1600 and 1604 for the Children of the Queen's Revels and then acquired by the King's Men and presented, with additional material, at the Globe Theatre in London.

The central figure is the deposed Duke of Genoa, Giovanni Altofronto who, in his disguise as the malcontent, Malevole, manages to remain an active force in the society from which he has been excluded, commenting throughout with detached cynicism on the hypocrisy and corruption of the Court. The villain of the piece is Mendoza who, having successfully plotted the downfall of Altofronto, rejoices in his role as favourite to Pietro Iacomo – the new Duke of Genoa. AURELIA, Duchess to Pietro, is easily seduced by Mendoza, but when she hears that he is unfaithful to her, discards him and takes the young courtier Ferneze to be her lover. Mendoza arranges Ferneze's death and finds his way back into AURELIA's favour. Then he orders Malevole to kill the Duke and Malevole pretends to have done so.

In this scene, Mendoza has inherited the Dukedom for himself and sends AURELIA into banishment. She enters, heavily guarded and supported by Celso and Ferrardo. She mourns the supposed death of Pietro, remembering his love for her and repenting her infidelity.

Act 4, Scene 5

AURELIA

Why? Why? I can desire nothing but death,
Nor deserve anything but hell.
If heaven should give sufficiency of grace
To clear my soul, it would make heaven graceless;
My sins would make the stock of mercy poor,
O, they would tire heaven's goodness to reclaim them.
Judgement is just, yet from that vast villain;
But sure, he shall not miss sad punishment
'Fore he shall rule. On to my cell of shame! . . .
O heaven!
As the soul loved the body, so loved he;
'Twas death to him to part my presence,
Heaven to see me pleased.
Yet I, like to a wretch given o'er to hell,
Brake all the sacred rites of marriage,
To clip a base, ungentle, faithless villain;
O God, a very pagan reprobate! –
What should I say? Ungrateful, throws me out,
For whom I lost soul, body, fame, and honour.
But 'tis most fit. Why should a better fate
Attend on any who forsake chaste sheets,
Fly the embrace of a devoted heart,
Joined by a solemn vow 'fore God and man,
To taste the brackish blood of beastly lust
In an adulterous touch? O ravenous immodesty,
Insatiate impudence of appetite!
Look, here's your end; for mark what sap in dust,
What sin in good, even so much love in lust.
Joy to thy ghost, sweet lord, pardon to me.

yet even though
sad heavy
brackish salty, licentious
immodesty excess
impudence shamelessness

The Plain Dealer

William Wycherley

First performed in 1676 at the Theatre Royal, London, this Restoration comedy attacks the double-dealing of Wycherley's society, and in particular the malicious gossip, the perversion of justice and theatre audiences who make out to be shocked at the so called obscenities in a play, but cannot wait to divulge the titillating details to their friends. The action revolves around Captain Manly, the 'plain dealer' of the title, who is described as honest, surly and having chosen a life at sea in order to avoid the world. He is in love with OLIVIA, who pretends to hate the 'lying, masking world' as much as he does, but at heart is affected, prudish and deceitful.

In this scene, OLIVIA is entertaining her cousin, Eliza, and her friends, Master Novel and Lord Plausible. As reputations are torn to shreds the conversation turns to Mr Wycherley's recent play, *The Country Wife*. OLIVIA expresses her disgust that 'Mistress Trifle' was seen in the audience on the second night and, despite her cousin's protestations, insists on relaying some of the play's more 'horrid' aspects.

Act 2, Scene 1

OLIVIA

[*To Lord Plausible*]

Then you think a woman modest that sees the hideous *Country Wife* without blushing or publishing her detestation of it? D'ye hear him, cousin? . . . [*To Eliza*] O fie fie fie, would you put me to blush anew, call all the blood into my face again? But to satisfy you then; first, the clandestine obscenity in the very name of Horner . . . Does it not give you the rank conception or image of a goat, a town-bull, or a satyr? Nay, what is yet a filthier image than all the rest, that of an eunuch? . . . Ay; but cousin one cannot stop there . . . O no, for when you have those filthy creatures in your head once, the next thing you think is what they do; as their defiling of honest men's beds and couches, rapes upon sleeping and waking country virgins under hedges and on haycocks; nay farther – . . . O, believe me, 'tis a filthy play; and you may take my word for a filthy play as soon as another's. But the filthiest thing in that play, or any other play, is – . . . No, faith, you shall know it; I'm resolved to make you out of love with the play. I say the lewdest, filthiest thing is his china; nay, I will never forgive the beastly author his china. He has quite taken away the reputation of poor china itself, and sullied the most innocent and pretty furniture of a lady's chamber, insomuch that I was fain to break all my defiled vessels. You see I have none left; nor you, I hope . . . Why, you will not keep any now, sure! 'Tis now as unfit an ornament for a lady's chamber as the pictures that come from Italy and other hot countries, as appears by their nudities, which I always cover or scratch out, whereso'er I find 'em. But china! Out upon't, filthy china, nasty, debauched china!

Horner i.e. cuckold-maker; by feigning impotence, Horner gains ready access to eager wives without sullying their reputations or arousing their husbands' jealousy

town-bull a bull communally owned by the cow-keepers of a village; hence 'one that rides all the women he meets'

haycocks conical heaps of hay in the field

furniture ornaments

pictures . . . Italy pornographic drawings after Giulio Romano's illustrations to Aretino's *Sonnetti Lussoriosi*

The Provoked Wife

John Vanbrugh

First performed at the New Theatre in Lincoln's Inn Fields, London, in 1697, this Restoration comedy is set in fashionable London and revolves around the unsuitable marriage of Sir John and LADY BRUTE and their separate efforts to reach some sort of compromise. In this opening scene, Sir John is bewailing his married state when LADY BRUTE enters and they immediately start quarrelling. Sir John accuses her of marrying him for his money and goes out, leaving LADY BRUTE to complain about her unhappy situation and her husband's brutish manners.

Act 1, Scene 1

LADY BRUTE

The devil's in the fellow, I think! – I was told before I married him that thus 'twould be. But I thought I had charms enough to govern him, and that where there was an estate a woman must needs be happy; so my vanity has deceived me, and my ambition has made me uneasy. But some comfort still; if one would be revenged of him, these are good times; a woman may have a gallant and a separate maintenance too. – The surly puppy! – Yet he's a fool for't, for hitherto he has been no monster. But who knows how far he may provoke me? I never loved him, yet I have been ever true to him; and that, in spite of all the attacks of art and nature upon a poor weak woman's heart in favour of a tempting lover. Methinks so noble a defence as I have made should be rewarded with a better usage. – Or who can tell? – Perhaps a good part of what I suffer from my husband may be a judgment upon me for my cruelty to my lover. – Lord, with what pleasure could I indulge that thought, were there but a possibility of finding arguments to make it good! – And how do I know but there may? Let me see. – What opposes? My matrimonial vow. – Why, what did I vow? I think I promised to be true to my husband. Well; and he promised to be kind to me. But he han't kept his word. – Why then, I'm absolved from mine. Ay, that seems clear to me. The argument's good between the king and the people, why not between the husband and the wife? – Oh, but that condition was not expressed. – No matter; 'twas understood. Well, by all I see, if I argue the matter a little longer with myself, I shan't find so many bugbears in the way as I thought I should. Lord, what fine notions of virtue do we women take up upon the credit of old foolish philosophers! Virtue's its own reward, virtue's this, virtue's that – virtue's an ass, and a gallant's worth forty on't.

monster cuckold

The Provoked Wife

John Vanbrugh

First performed at the New Theatre in Lincoln's Inn Fields, London, in 1697, this Restoration comedy is set in fashionable London and revolves around the unsuitable marriage of Sir John and Lady Brute and their separate efforts to reach some sort of compromise. LADY FANCYFULL, a frequent visitor to the house, is the laughing stock of Lady Brute and her friends, with her coquettish airs and affected mannerisms. So much so that Heartfree, a man to whom she is attracted but who is indifferent to her charms, has felt it his duty to point out her faults to her. In this scene, LADY FANCYFULL tells the assembled company how 'fatigued' she is with the 'addresses' of so many gentlemen. She singles out Heartfree as her adviser, as he has been so good as to enumerate her many faults.

Act 3, Scene 1

LADY FANCYFULL

My dear lady Brute! And sweet Bellinda! Methinks 'tis an age since I saw you ... Why really, to confess the truth to you, I am so everlastingly fatigued with the addresses of unfortunate gentlemen, that were it not for the extravagancy of the example I should e'en tear out these wicked eyes with my own fingers, to make both myself and mankind easy. – What think you on't, Mr Heartfree, for I take you to be my faithful adviser? ... Would you believe it, ladies? The gentleman has been so exceeding generous, to tell me of above fifty faults in less time than it was well possible for me to commit two of 'em ... He has had the goodness to design a reformation, even down to my fingers' ends. – 'Twas thus, I think, sir, you would have had 'em stand. [*Opening her fingers in an awkward manner*] – My eyes, too, he did not like. – How was't you would have directed 'em? Thus, I think. [*Staring at him*] – Then there was something amiss in my gait, too; I don't know well how 'twas, but as I take it he would have had me walk like him. – Pray, sir, do me the favour to take a turn or two about the room, that the company may see you. – He's sullen, ladies, and won't. But, to make short, and give you as true an idea as I can of the matter, I think 'twas much about this figure in general he would have moulded me to. [*She walks awkwardly about, staring and looking ungainly, then changes on a sudden to the extremity of her usual affectation*] But I was an obstinate woman, and could not resolve to make myself mistress of his heart by growing as awkward as his fancy.

The Provoked Wife

John Vanbrugh

First performed at the New Theatre in Lincoln's Inn Fields, London, in 1697, this Restoration comedy is set in fashionable London and revolves around the unsuitable marriage of Sir John and Lady Brute and their separate efforts to reach some sort of compromise. For almost two years, Constant has been courting Lady Brute, although so far she has never given him the least sign of encouragement. Now she and her niece BELLINDA invite him and his friend Heartfree to join them for an evening at cards. Sir John arrives home unexpectedly and the two men take refuge in the closet. Sir John discovers them, accuses his wife of cuckolding him and then collapses into a drunken stupor. This gives them time to think up a story and in this speech BELLINDA outlines her plan.

Act 5, Scene 2

BELLINDA

'Tis well he is so, that we may have time to lay our story handsomely; for we must lie like the devil to bring ourselves off ... I'll tell you: it must all light upon Heartfree and I. We'll say he has courted me some time, but for reasons unknown to us has ever been very earnest the thing might be kept from Sir John; that therefore hearing him upon the stairs, he run into the closet, though against our will, and Constant with him, to prevent jealousy. And to give this a good impudent face of truth (that I may deliver you from the trouble you are in), I'll e'en (if he pleases) marry him ... I like him, and have fortune enough to keep above extremity. I can't say I would live with him in a cell upon love and bread and butter; but I had rather have the man I love, and a middle state of life, than that gentleman in the chair there, and twice your ladyship's splendour ... Some risk, I do confess, there always is; but if a man has the least spark either of honour or good nature, he can never use a woman ill that loves him and makes his fortune both. Yet I must own to you, some little struggling I still have with this teasing ambition of ours; for pride, you know is as natural to a woman as 'tis to a saint. I can't help being fond of this rogue; and yet it goes to my heart to think I must never whisk to Hyde Park with above a pair of horses, have no coronet upon my coach, nor a page to carry up my train. But above all, that business of place – . Well, taking place is a noble prerogative ... But pray say no more on't, for fear I change my mind. For o'my conscience, were't not for your affair in the balance, I should go near to pick up some odious man of quality yet, and only take poor Heartfree for a gallant.

place social precedence

87

The Relapse

John Vanbrugh

This Restoration comedy was first performed in 1696 at the Theatre Royal, Drury Lane in London. The action revolves around the reconciliation of the virtuous AMANDA and her profligate husband, Loveless, who, although he has begged forgiveness and sworn undying love, immediately falls for his wife's beautiful cousin, Berinthia. As the affair develops Berinthia hints to AMANDA that Loveless is involved with an unknown woman and urges her to revenge herself by accepting the advances of Berinthia's friend Worthy, but AMANDA is determined to remain virtuous. In this scene, AMANDA has just witnessed a meeting, set up by Berinthia, of her husband and a 'masked woman' – Berinthia herself. Shocked and upset, she angrily dismisses her maid, and once alone, considers her position and what action to take.

Act 5, Scene 4

AMANDA
Would the world were on fire, and you in the middle on't!
Begone. Leave me – [*Exit Woman*]
At last I am convinced. My eyes are testimonies of his
falsehood. The base, ungrateful, perjured villain! –
Good gods! What slippery stuff are men compos'd of!
Sure the account of their creation's false,
And 'twas the woman's rib that they were form'd of.
But why am I thus angry?
This poor relapse should only move my scorn.
'Tis true, the roving flights of his unfinished youth
Had strong excuse from the plea of nature;
Reason had thrown the reins loose on his neck,
And slipped him to unlimited desire.
If therefore he went wrong, he had a claim
To my forgiveness, and I did him right.
But since the years of manhood rein him in,
And reason, well digested into thought,
Has pointed out the course he ought to run;
If now he strays,
'Twould be as weak and mean in me to pardon,
As it had been in him t'offend. But hold:
'Tis an ill cause indeed, where nothing's to be said for't.
My beauty possibly is in the wane;
Perhaps sixteen has greater charms for him:
Yes, there's the secret. But let him know,
My quiver's not entirely emptied yet,
I still have darts, and I can shoot 'em too;
They're not so blunt, but they can enter still:
The want's not in my power, but in my will.
Virtue's his friend; or, through another's heart,
I yet could find the way to make his smart.
                              [*Going off, she meets Worthy*]
Ha! he here?
Protect me, heaven, for this looks ominous.

The Revenger's Tragedy

Anon

The authorship of this play remains uncertain. Registered in the Stationer's Registry in 1607 and performed by His Majesty's Servants, it is possibly an episode in the history of the Medici family. Early in the play the DUCHESS' younger son has been accused of rape, a crime punishable by death. The elderly Duke, the boy's stepfather, could have easily secured his release, but declines to do so, deferring the sentencing to a later date. In this scene the DUCHESS determines to take revenge on her husband by seducing Spurio, the Duke's bastard son.

Act 1, Scene 2

DUCHESS
Was't ever known step-duchess was so mild
And calm as I? Some now would plot his death
With easy doctors, those loose living men,
And make his withered Grace fall to his grave
And keep church better.
Some second wife would do this, and dispatch
Her double loathèd lord at meat and sleep.
Indeed 'tis true an old man's twice a child,
Mine cannot speak! One of his single words
Would quite have freed my youngest dearest son
From death or durance, and have made him walk
With a bold foot upon the thorny law,
Whose prickles should bow under him; but 't 'as not:
And therefore wedlock faith shall be forgot.
I'll kill him in his forehead, hate there feed –
That wound is deepest though it never bleed;
[*Enter Spurio*]
And here comes he whom my heart points unto,
His bastard son, but my love's true-begot;
Many a wealthy letter have I sent him
Swelled up with jewels, and the timorous man
Is yet but coldly kind;
That jewel's mine that quivers in his ear,
Mocking his master's chilliness and vain fear –
H'as spied me now.

easy compliant
durance imprisonment

The Rivals

Richard Brinsley Sheridan

This eighteenth-century comedy of manners was first performed at the Theatre Royal, Covent Garden, London, in 1775. It is set in Bath and revolves around the rivals for the hand of the lovely Lydia Languish and the subsequent intrigues leading up to a comic attempt at a duel. In this early scene, LYDIA's cousin Julia has just arrived in Bath, and LYDIA is anxious to impart the latest news, before they are interrupted by her aunt, Mrs Malaprop.

Act 1, Scene 2

LYDIA

Ah! Julia, I have a thousand things to tell you! . . . Before we are interrupted, let me impart to you some of my distress! I know your gentle nature will sympathize with me, though your prudence may condemn me! My letters have informed you of my whole connection with Beverley – but I have lost him, Julia! – my aunt has discovered our intercourse by a note she intercepted, and has confined me ever since! – Yet, would you believe it? she has fallen absolutely in love with a tall Irish baronet she met one night since we have been here, at Lady Macshuffle's rout . . . No, upon my word. She really carries on a kind of correspondence with him, under a feigned name though, till she chooses to be known to him – but it is a *Delia* or a *Celia*, I assure you . . . Since she has discovered her own frailty, she is become more suspicious of mine. Then I must inform you of another plague! That odious Acres is to be in Bath today; so that I protest I shall be teased out of all spirits! . . . But you have not heard the worst. Unfortunately I had quarrelled with my poor Beverley, just before my aunt made the discovery, and I have not seen him since, to make it up . . . I don't know how it was, as often as we had been together, we had never had a quarrel! And, somehow I was afraid he would never give me an opportunity. So, last Thursday, I wrote a letter to myself, to inform myself that Beverley was at that time paying his addresses to another woman. I signed it *your Friend unknown*, showed it to Beverley, charged him with his falsehood, put myself in a violent passion, and vowed I'd never see him more . . . 'Twas the next day my aunt found the matter out. I intended only to have teased him three days and a half, and now I've lost him for ever.

rout party, social gathering

The Rivals

Richard Brinsley Sheridan

This eighteenth-century comedy of manners was first performed at the Theatre Royal, Covent Garden, London, in 1775. It is set in Bath and revolves around the rivals for the hand of the lovely Lydia Languish and the subsequent intrigues leading up to a comic attempt at a duel. In this scene Lydia's aunt, MRS MALA-PROP, who considers herself 'Queen of the dictionary' and is continually mispronouncing her words, is attempting to arrange a marriage for her niece with Captain Absolute, son of her friend Sir Anthony, but Lydia stubbornly refuses to listen, insisting that she will never give up her beloved 'Ensign Beverley'.

Act 1, Scene 2

MRS MALAPROP

There, Sir Anthony, there sits the deliberate simpleton, who wants to disgrace her family, and lavish herself on a fellow not worth a shilling! . . . You thought, Miss! I don't know any business you have to think at all – thought does not become a young woman; the point we would request of you is, that you will promise to forget this fellow – to illiterate him, I say, quite from your memory . . . there is nothing on earth so easy as to *forget*, if a person chooses to set about it. I'm sure I have as much forgot your poor dear uncle as if he had never existed – and I thought it my duty so to do; and let me tell you, Lydia, these violent memories don't become a young woman . . . Now don't attempt to extirpate yourself from the matter; you know I have proof controvertible of it. But tell me, will you promise to do as you're bid? Will you take a husband of your friend's choosing? . . . What business have you, Miss, with *preference* and *aversion*? They don't become a young woman; and you ought to know, that as both always wear off, 'tis safest in matrimony to begin with a little aversion. I am sure I hated your poor dear uncle before marriage as if he'd been a blackamoor – and yet, Miss, you are sensible what a wife I made! – and when it pleased Heaven to release me from him, 'tis unknown what tears I shed! But suppose we were going to give you another choice, will you promise us to give up this Beverley? . . . Take yourself to your room. You are fit company for nothing but your own ill-humours. . . . [*Exit* Lydia] There's a little intricate hussy for you!

illiterate for, obliterate
forgot i.e. forgotten (a possible eighteenth-century usage)
extirpate root out or exterminate: for, extricate or exculpate
controvertible for, incontrovertible
friend's relation's
sensible aware
intricate perplexed or complicated: for, ingrate?

The Rover

Aphra Behn

First performed in 1677 at the Duke's Theatre, London, this Restoration comedy is set in the 1650s in Naples during carnival time. In England, Cromwell's Protectorate had suppressed such bawdy activities, but abroad a young Englishman was free to enjoy himself in a way he could never hope to at home.

The action centres around Willimore – 'The Rover' – or wanderer, who steps ashore in search of 'love and mirth'. Among his amorous adventures he becomes involved with the famous courtesan ANGELLICA BIANCA, who despite the warnings of her woman, Moretta, falls in love with him. She discovers he has betrayed her and, in this scene, holds him at pistol point in order to revenge her honour. Although the play is written in prose, note that ANGELLICA's speech is in blank verse.

Act 5, Scene 1

ANGELLICA
Behold this face – so lost to thy remembrance!
[*Pulls off her vizard*]
And then call all thy sins about thy soul,
And let 'em die with thee . . .
Yes, traitor,
Does not thy guilty blood run shivering through thy veins?
Hast thou no horror at this sight that tells thee
Thou has not long to boast thy shameful conquest?
                                        . . . Tell me,
How many poor believing fools thou hast undone?
How many hearts thou hast betrayed to ruin?
– Yet these are little mischiefs to the ills
Thou'st taught mine to commit: thou'st taught it love! . . .

Love, that has robbed it of its unconcern,
Of all that pride that taught me how to value it.
And in its room
A mean submissive passion was conveyed,
That made me humbly bow, which I ne'er did
To anything but Heaven.
Thou, perjured man, didst this, and with thy oaths,
Which on thy knees thou didst devoutly make,
Softened my yielding heart – and then, I was a slave.
– Yet still had been content to've worn my chains,
Worn 'em with vanity and joy forever,
Had'st thou not broke those vows that put them on.
'Twas then I was undone.
        [*All this while follows him with the pistol to his breast*] . . .
Had I remained in innocent security,
I should have thought all men were born my slaves,
And worn my power like lightning in my eyes,
To have destroyed at pleasure when offended.
But when love held the mirror, the undeceiving glass
Reflected all the weakness of my soul, and made me know
My richest treasure being lost, my honour,
All the remaining spoil could not be worth
The conqueror's care or value.
Oh, how I fell like a long-worshipped idol,
Discovering all the cheat.
Would not the incense and rich sacrifice
Which blind devotion offered at my altars
Have fallen to thee?
Why would'st thou then destroy my fancied power?

The School for Scandal

Richard Brinsley Sheridan

This comedy of manners was first performed at Drury Lane, London, in 1777 and is set in fashionable London. At the centre of the play is the group of scandal mongers – 'The School' – who meet on a regular basis to tear the reputations of their friends and relatives to pieces and, as in the whispering game, the scandals grow more and more preposterous.

In this opening scene in Lady Sneerwell's dressing-room, MRS CANDOUR, described by her hostess as 'a little talkative' but the 'best sort of woman', pays her regular call, bringing in the latest gossip for the 'School' to get their teeth into.

Act 1, Scene 1

MRS CANDOUR

My dear Lady Sneerwell, how have you been this century? Mr Surface, what news do you hear? Though indeed it is no matter, for I think one hears nothing else but scandal . . . Ah, Maria, child! What, is the whole affair off between you and Charles? His extravagance, I presume? The town talks of nothing else . . . but there's no stopping people's tongues. I own I was hurt to hear it, as indeed I was to learn from the same quarter that your guardian, Sir Peter, and Lady Teazle have not agreed lately as well as could be wished . . . But what's to be done? People *will* talk; there's no preventing it. Why it was but yesterday I was told that Miss Gadabout had eloped with Sir Filigree Flirt. But, Lord, there's no minding what one hears – though to be sure I had this from very good authority . . . But the world is so censorious, no character escapes. Lord, now who would have suspected your friend Miss Prim of an indiscretion? Yet such is the ill nature of people that they say her uncle stopped her last week just as she was stepping into the York diligence with her dancing-master . . . Oh, no foundation in the world, I dare swear. No more probably than for the story circulated last month of Mrs Festino's affair with Colonel Cassino – though to be sure that matter was never rightly cleared up . . . Tale-bearers are as bad as the tale-makers – 'tis an old observation, and a very true one. But what's to be done, as I said before? How will you prevent people from talking? Today Mrs Clackitt assured me Mr and Mrs Honeymoon were at last become mere man and wife like the rest of their acquaintance. She likewise hinted that a certain widow in the next street had got rid of her dropsy and recovered her shape in a most surprising manner. And at the same time Miss Tattle, who was by, affirmed that Lord Buffalo had discovered his lady at a house of no extraordinary fame – and that Sir Harry Bouquet and Tom Saunter were to measure swords on a similar provocation. But, Lord, do you think I would report these things? No, no, tale-bearers, as I said before, are just as bad as the tale-makers . . . I confess, Mr Surface, I cannot bear to hear people attacked behind their backs, and when ugly circumstances come out against one's acquaintance, I own I always love to think the best. By the bye, I hope 'tis not true your brother is absolutely ruined?

She Stoops to Conquer

Oliver Goldsmith

This eighteenth-century comedy was first produced at the Theatre Royal, Covent Garden, London, in 1773. It is set in the Hardcastles' country mansion and parodies the sentimental comedies popular at that time. Mr Hardcastle and his friend, Sir Charles Marlow, have arranged a match between the Hardcastles' daughter, Kate, and Young Marlow. In this scene Young Marlow and his friend Hastings have arrived from London and MRS HARDCASTLE is anxious to have news of the latest London fashions and gossip. She is flirtatious and over-bearing, determined to impress Young Marlow with her superior manners and dress sense.

Act 2, Scene 1

MRS HARDCASTLE

Well! I vow, Mr Hastings, you are very entertaining. There's nothing in the world I love to talk of so much as London, and the fashions, though I was never there myself . . . Oh! Sir, you're only pleased to say so. We country persons can have no manner at all. I'm in love with the town, and that serves to raise me above some of our neighbouring rustics; but who can have a manner, that has never seen the Pantheon, the Grotto Gardens, the Borough, and such places where the Nobility chiefly resort? All I can do, is to enjoy London at second-hand. I take care to know every tête-à-tête from the *Scandalous Magazine*, and have all the fashions, as they come out, in a letter from the two Miss Rickets of Crooked Lane. Pray how do you like this head, Mr Hastings? . . . I protest I dressed it myself from a print in the *Ladies Memorandum-book* for the last year . . . I vow, since inoculation began, there is no such thing to be seen as a plain woman; so one must dress a little particular or one may escape in the crowd . . . Yet, what signifies *my* dressing when I have such a piece of antiquity by my side as Mr Hardcastle: all I can say will never argue down a single button from his clothes. I have often wanted him to throw off his great flaxen wig, and where he was bald, to plaster it over like my Lord Pately, with powder . . . But what do you think his answer was? Why, with his usual Gothic vivacity, he said I only wanted him to throw off his wig to convert it into a *tête* for my own wearing . . . Pray, Mr Hastings, what do you take to be the most fashionable age about town? Seriously? Then I shall be too young for the fashion.

manner a fashionable air (1694)
head her hair has been elaborately built up over a stuffed frame (1494)
inoculation against smallpox, a general practice by 1722, (half a century before, that is)
tête tall, elaborate hair-piece – 'head' (1756)

She Stoops to Conquer

Oliver Goldsmith

This eighteenth-century comedy was first produced at the Theatre Royal, Covent Garden, London, in 1773. It is set in the Hardcastles' country mansion and parodies the sentimental comedies popular at that time. The action revolves around the match between MISS HARDCASTLE and the reserved Young Marlow, arranged by their respective fathers. Here MISS HARD-CASTLE, witty and lively, having 'stooped to conquer' by pretending to be her father's serving wench in order to overcome Marlow's shyness with women of his own class, speaks the epilogue. It is written in rhymed couplets.

Epilogue

MISS HARDCASTLE
Well, having stooped to conquer with success,
And gained a husband without aid from dress,
Still as a Barmaid, I could wish it too,
As I have conquered him to conquer you:
And let me say, for all your resolution,
That pretty Barmaids have done execution.
Our life is all a play, composed to please,
We have our exits and our entrances.
The first act shows the simple country maid,
Harmless and young, of every thing afraid;
Blushes when hired, and with unmeaning action,
'I hopes as how to give you satisfaction'.
Her second act displays a livelier scene. –
Th'unblushing Barmaid of a country inn.
Who whisks about the house, at market caters,
Talks loud, coquets the guests, and scolds the waiters.

102

Next the scene shifts to town, and there she soars,
The chop house toast of ogling connoisseurs.
On Squires and Cits she there displays her arts,
And on the gridiron broils her lovers' hearts –
And as she smiles, her triumphs to complete,
Even Common Councilmen forget to eat.
The fourth act shows her wedded to the Squire,
And Madam now begins to hold it higher;
Pretends to taste, at Operas cries, *Caro*,
And quits her Nancy Dawson, for *Che faro*.
Dotes upon dancing, and in all her pride,
Swims round the room, the *Heinel* of Cheapside:
Ogles and leers with artificial skill,
Till having lost in age the power to kill,
She sits all night at cards, and ogles at spadille.
Such, through our lives, the eventful history –
The fifth and last act still remains for me.
The Barmaid now for your protection prays,
Turns Female Barrister, and pleads for Bayes.

Cit 'a pert low townsman'

Caro dear (Italian); hence, excellent, superb

spadille the name for 'the ace of spades at ombre', a card game (1728)

Nancy Dawson . . . Che faro. Nancy Dawson was a famous hornpipe dancer, who had a song named after her; 'che farò senza Euridice' the famous aria from Act III of Gluck's opera *Orfeo ed Euridice* (1762).

Heinel Anna-Frederica Heinel, a famous dancer who appeared in the interludes that were a feature of the opera.

Barrister . . . Bayes Mr Bayes, the hero of Buckingham's *Rehearsal*, became a stock name for a dramatist; with a pun on 'bays', the laurel crown for poetry, and another, rather feeble one on barmaid/barrister.

The Shoemaker's Holiday

Thomas Dekker

This London comedy was most likely first performed at the Rose Theatre, London, in the late summer or autumn of 1599. It tells the story of Simon Eyre, a Shoemaker, who, through his hard work and popularity amongst his workers and their families, rises to become Lord Mayor of London.

At the beginning of the play, Roland Lacy, nephew of the Earl of Lincoln and later employed by Eyre as 'Hans', a Dutch Shoemaker, is being sent to join the army in France. His sweetheart, Rose, daughter of the present Lord Mayor, is heartbroken at their parting. In this scene, set in the Lord Mayor's country mansion at Old Ford, Rose's spirited Maid, SYBIL, brings news of Lacy from London. She comments sardonically on his extravagant attire and haughty manner, suggesting to her young mistress that she would be far better off without him.

Scene 2

SYBIL

By my troth, I scant knew him – here 'a wore a scarf, and here a scarf, here a bunch of feathers, and here precious stones and jewels, and a pair of garters – O monstrous! – like one of our yellow silk curtains at home here in Old Ford House, here in Master Bellymount's chamber. I stood at our door in Cornhill, looked at him, he at me indeed; spake to him, but he not to me, not a word. Marry gup, thought I, with a wanion! He passed by me as proud – Marry, foh! Are you grown humorous? thought I – and so shut the door, and in I came ... Mild? Yea, as a bushel of stamped crabs! He looked upon me as sour as verjuice. Go thy ways, thought I, thou mayst be much in my gaskins, but nothing in my netherstocks. This is your fault, mistress, to love him that loves not you. He thinks scorn to do as he's done to, but if I were as you,

I'd cry: go by, Jeronimo, go by!
I'd set mine old debts against my new driblets,
And the hare's foot against the goose giblets;
For if ever I sigh when sleep I should take,
Pray God I may lose my maidenhead when I wake ...

By my troth, he is a proper man, but he is proper that proper doth. Let him go snick up, young mistress.

Marry gup My, aren't we getting above ourselves?

wanion vengeance

humorous moody

bushel measure of eight gallons

stamped crabs crab-apples crushed for their sour juice

verjuice juice of unripe fruit, used in cooking

gaskins ... netherstocks breeches ... stockings; i.e. though I may be outwardly civil to you, don't imagine we are intimate friends.

Go by, Jeronimo, go by a hackneyed phrase derived from Kyd's hugely popular play *The Spanish Tragedy* (c. 1598), meaning 'be off with you!'

I'd ... giblets proverbial expressions, urging Rose to consider what she's letting herself in for

driblets petty debts

sign i.e. for a man

proper handsome

snick up hang

The Spanish Tragedy

Thomas Kyd

Written sometime between 1582 and 1592 and performed in London by Lord Strange's Men for theatrical entrepreneur Philip Henslowe in February 1592, it is one of the earlier Elizabethan revenge tragedies.

Overseeing the main action is the ghost of Don Andrea, seeking revenge for his death in battle at the hands of Don Balthazar, Prince of Portingale*. He is accompanied by the personification of 'Revenge', who promises him vengeance and the opportunity to watch the tortuous route by which his enemy reaches his inevitable destruction. Hieronimo, Knight Marshal of Spain, and his wife, ISABELLA, have discovered their son, Horatio, hanging in the arbour next to their house, brutally murdered. Hieronimo cuts his son's body down, but is too late to prevent ISABELLA seeing his mutilated corpse.

In this scene we witness the beginning of ISABELLA's madness. Her maid is trying to console her, offering herbs and soothing medicines, but 'she runs lunatic'.

* Portugal

Act 3, Scene 8

ISABELLA

So that, you say, this herb will purge the eye,
And this the head?
Ah, but none of them will purge the heart:
No, there's no medicine left for my disease,
Nor any physic to recure the dead.

She runs lunatic

Horatio! O, where's Horatio? . . .
Why, did I not give you gowns and goodly things,
Bought you a whistle and a whipstalk, too,
To be revenged on their villainies? . . .
My soul! poor soul, thou talks of things
Thou know'st not what – my soul hath silver wings,
That mounts me up unto the highest heavens;
To heaven, ay, there sits my Horatio,
Backed with a troop of fiery cherubins,
Dancing about his newly-healed wounds,
Singing sweet hymns and chanting heavenly notes,
Rare harmony to greet his innocence,
That died, ay died a mirror in our days.
But say, where shall I find the men, the murderers,
That slew Horatio? Whither shall I run
To find them out that murdered my son?

[*Exeunt*]

---

purge cleanse, heal
recure recover, restore to health
whipstalk whip-handle; used, presumably, in a child's game
mirror model of excellence

The Spanish Tragedy

Thomas Kyd

Written sometime between 1582 and 1592 and performed in London by Lord Strange's Men for theatrical entrepreneur Philip Henslowe in February 1592, it is one of the earlier Elizabethan revenge tragedies.

Overseeing the main action is the ghost of Don Andrea, seeking revenge for his death in battle at the hands of Don Balthazar, Prince of Portingale*. He is accompanied by the personification of 'Revenge', who promises him vengeance and the opportunity to watch the tortuous route by which his enemy reaches his inevitable destruction. BEL-IMPERIA, beautiful daughter of the Duke of Castile and formerly betrothed to Andrea, turned for comfort after his death to his friend Horatio, who became her 'second love'. Balthazar, determined to win BEL-IMPERIA for himself, together with her brother, Lorenzo, waylays the two lovers at their meeting place, abducts BEL-IMPERIA and brutally murders Horatio. Now on her father's insistence, BEL-IMPERIA is being forced to marry Balthazar.

In this scene she appeals to Horatio's father for help, berating him for his seeming friendship with her lover's murderers.

* Portugal

Act 4, Scene 1

BEL-IMPERIA

Is this the love thou bear'st Horatio?
Is this the kindness that thou counterfeits?
Are these the fruits of thine incessant tears?
Hieronimo, are these thy passions,
Thy protestations and thy deep laments,
That thou wert wont to weary men withal?
O unkind father, O deceitful world!
With what excuses canst thou show thyself,
What what . . . .
From this dishonour and the hate of men? –
Thus to neglect the loss and life of him
Whom both my letters and thine own belief
Assures thee to be causeless slaughtered.
Hieronimo, for shame, Hieronimo,
Be not a history to after times
Of such ingratitude unto thy son.
Unhappy mothers of such children then –
But monstrous fathers, to forget so soon
The death of those, whom they with care and cost
Have tendered so, thus careless should be lost.
Myself a stranger in respect of thee,
So loved his life, as still I wish their deaths;
Nor shall his death be unrevenged by me,
Although I bear it out for fashion's sake:
For here I swear in sight of heaven and earth,
Shouldst thou neglect the love thou shouldst retain
And give it over and devise no more,
Myself should send their hateful souls to hell,
That wrought his downfall with extremest death.

passions passionate exclamations
unkind unnatural
history example, tale
tendered cared for, cherished
in respect of compared to
bear it . . . sake 'make pretence of accepting the situation for the sake of appearances'
devise plot
extremest most cruel

'Tis Pity She's a Whore

John Ford

First published in 1633 and performed by the Queen's Company at the Phoenix in Drury Lane, London, sometime between 1629 and 1633. HIPPOLITA, wife of Richardetto, has been seduced by the nobleman Soranzo with vows of love and promises of marriage. He has even encouraged her to send her husband on a mission resulting in his supposed 'death'. Now he has discarded her for the merchant's daughter, Annabella, and in this scene she forces her way into his study and confronts him with his betrayal.

Act 2, Scene 2

HIPPOLITA
'Tis I:
Do you know me now? Look, perjured man, on her
Whom thou and thy distracted lust have wronged.
Thy sensual rage of blood hath made my youth
A scorn to men and angels, and shall I
Be now a foil to thy unsated change?
Thou knowst, false wanton, when my modest fame
Stood free from stain or scandal, all the charms
Of hell or sorcery could not prevail
Against the honour of my chaster bosom.
Thine eyes did plead in tears, thy tongue in oaths
Such and so many, that a heart of steel
Would have been wrought to pity, as was mine:
And shall the conquest of my lawful bed,
My husband's death urged on by his disgrace,
My loss of womanhood, be ill rewarded
With hatred and contempt? No; know, Soranzo,
I have a spirit doth as much distaste
The slavery of fearing thee, as thou
Dost loathe the memory of what hath passed.
                             ... Call me not dear,
Nor think with supple words to smooth the grossness
Of my abuses; 'tis not your new mistress,
Your goodly Madam Merchant, shall triumph
On my dejection: tell her thus from me,
My birth was nobler and by much more free.
                             ... You are too double
In your dissimulation. Seest thou this,
This habit, these black mourning weeds of care?
'Tis thou art cause of this, and hast divorced
My husband from his life and me from him,
And made me widow in my widowhood.

foil ... change background for your promiscuity
distaste dislike
triumph accented on second syllable

Volpone

Ben Jonson

First performed in London in 1605 by the King's Men and set in Venice. Volpone, aided by his confederate, Mosca, sets out to dupe various legacy-hunters by pretending to be on his death-bed and promising to make each one of them his sole heir. They in turn, to keep in favour, bring him rich offerings, each trying to outvie potential rivals. One of these legacy-hunters, the merchant Corvino, offers him his young wife, CELIA. In this scene, CELIA, having been threatened by her husband with dire consequences if she doesn't please Volpone, is left alone at the 'sick man's' bedside. Volpone leaps out at her, offering himself as 'a worthy lover in place of a base husband' and promising her precious jewels, exquisite goods and a life of luxury if she will yield to him.

Act 3, Scene 7

CELIA

Good sir, these things might move a mind affected
With such delights; but I, whose innocence
Is all I can think wealthy, or worth th'enjoying,
And which once lost, I have nought to lose beyond it,
Cannot be taken with these sensual baits:
If you have conscience – . . .
If you have ears that will be pierced; or eyes,
That can be opened; a heart, may be touched;
Or any part, that yet sounds man, about you:
If you have touch of holy saints, or heaven,
Do me the grace, to let me scape. If not,
Be bountiful, and kill me. You do know,
I am a creature, hither ill betrayed,
By one, whose shame I would forget it were.
If you will deign me neither of these graces,
Yet feed your wrath, sir, rather than your lust;
(It is a vice, comes nearer manliness)
And punish that unhappy crime of nature,
Which you miscall my beauty: flay my face,
Or poison it, with ointments, for seducing
Your blood to this rebellion. Rub these hands,
With what may cause an eating leprosy,
E'en to my bones, and marrow: anything,
That may disfavour me, save in my honour.
And I will kneel to you, pray for you, pay down
A thousand hourly vows, sir, for your health,
Report, and think you virtuous –

disfavour disfigure

The Way of the World

William Congreve

This Restoration comedy was first presented at the Lincoln's Inn Fields Theatre, in London, in 1700 and set in fashionable London. The main action revolves around the courtship of the witty and vivacious MRS MILLAMANT – the name means 'she has a thousand lovers' – by the 'admirable' Edward Mirabell. Although MRS MILLAMANT indulges in the affected conversation and manners of the period and has many and various young admirers in attendance, she truly loves Mirabell. In this scene, having teased and skilfully kept him at arm's length throughout most of the play, she is cornered at last. She admits that she 'is on the verge of matrimony' but at the same time insists on setting out her conditions of marriage before finally capitulating.

Act 4, Scene 1

MRS MILLAMANT

My dear liberty, shall I leave thee? My faithful solitude, my darling contemplation, must I bid you then adieu? Ay-h, adieu; my morning thoughts, agreeable wakings, indolent slumbers, all ye *douceurs*, ye *sommeils du matin*, adieu? I can't do't, 'tis more than impossible. Positively, Mirabell, I'll lie a-bed in a morning as long as I please ... I won't be called names after I'm married; positively, I won't be called names ... Ay, as wife, spouse, my dear, joy, jewel, love, sweetheart, and the rest of that nauseous cant in which men and their wives are so fulsomely familiar. I shall never bear that. Good Mirabell, don't let us be familiar or fond, nor kiss before folks like my Lady Fadler and Sir Francis, nor go to Hyde Park together the first Sunday in a new chariot, to provoke eyes and whispers, and then never to be seen there together again; as if we were proud of one another the first week, and ashamed of one another for ever after. Let us never visit together, nor go to a play together, but let us be very strange and well-bred; let us be as strange as if we had been married a great while, and as well-bred as if we were not married at all ... Trifles – as, liberty to pay and receive visits to and from whom I please, to write and receive letters, without interrogatories or wry faces on your part; to wear what I please, and choose conversation with regard only to my own taste; to have no obligation upon me to converse with wits that I don't like, because they are your acquaintance, or to be intimate with fools, because they may be your relations. Come to dinner when I please, dine in my dressing-room when I'm out of humour, without giving a reason. To have my closet inviolate, to be sole empress of my tea table, which you must never presume to approach without first asking leave; and lastly, wherever I am, you shall always knock at the door before you come in. These articles subscribed, if I continue to endure you a little longer, I may by degrees dwindle into a wife.

---

nauseous Like 'filthy', the word is not used with the strong emphasis it has today; affected exaggeration of such words ('dreadful', 'terrible', 'catastrophic') remains a characteristic of modern affected speech, however.

Fadler one who indulges in fondling

strange reserved

The Way of the World

William Congreve

This Restoration comedy was first presented at the Lincoln's Inn Fields Theatre, in London, in 1700 and set in fashionable London. The main action is centred around the romance between LADY WISHFORT's niece Millamant and Edward Mirabell. The old lady detests Mirabell, supposing herself spurned by him and has no intention of sanctioning her niece's marriage or releasing the inheritance due to her. To make matters worse, she has just discovered that 'Sir Rowland' – who has been wooing her ardently with promises of marriage – is in actual fact Mirabell's servant Waitwell in disguise, and that her own servant Foible has been party to the deception. In this scene, Foible is making excuses and begging for forgiveness, but LADY WISHFORT orders her to leave the house immediately.

Act 5, Scene 1

LADY WISHFORT

Out of my house, out of my house, thou viper, thou serpent that I have fostered! Thou bosom traitress, that I raised from nothing, begone, begone, begone! Go! Go! That I took from washing of old gauze and weaving of dead hair, with a bleak blue nose, over a chafing dish of starved embers, and dining behind a traverse rag, in a shop no bigger than a birdcage! Go, go, starve again! Do! Do! ... Away, out, out! Go set up for yourself again! Do, drive a trade, do! With your threepennyworth of small ware, flaunting upon a packthread, under a brandy-seller's bulk, or against a dead wall by a ballad-monger! Go hang out an old frisoneer gorget, with a yard of yellow colberteen again, do! An old gnawed mask, two rows of pins and a child's fiddle, a glass necklace with the beads broken, and a quilted nightcap with one ear! Go, go, drive a trade! These were your

commodities, you treacherous trull, this was your merchandise you
dealt in, when I took you into my house, placed you next myself,
and made you governante of my whole family. You have forgot this,
have you, now you have feathered your nest? . . . No damage? What,
to betray me, to marry me to a cast servingman? To make me a
receptacle, an hospital for a decayed pimp? No damage? Oh thou
frontless impudence – more than a big-bellied actress . . . What, then
I have been your property, have I? I have been convenient to you, it
seems, while you were catering for Mirabell. I have been broker for
you! What, have you made a passive bawd of me? This exceeds all
precedent; I am brought to fine uses, to become a botcher of second-
hand marriages between Abigails and Andrews! I'll couple you, yes,
I'll baste you together, you and your Philander! I'll Duke's Place you,
as I'm a person! Your turtle is in custody already: you shall coo in
the same cage, if there be constable or warrant in the parish!

gauze thin transparent fabric, silk linen or cotton
weaving of dead hair making wigs
chafing dish vessel holding burning coal to warm dishes placed on it
traverse rag tattered curtain
bulk stall
dead wall a continuous wall, with the suggestion of monotony, dreariness, slum areas
ballad-monger a beggarly occupation
frisoneer gorget stiff neckpiece (French, *gorge*, throat) made of Friesland stuff
colberteen cheap lace
governante housekeeper
frontless shameless
broker second-hand dealer, hence procurer, pimp, bawd
Abigails and Andrews maidservants and manservants
baste flog
Philander lover
Duke's Place irregular marriages were notorious at St James's Church there

The White Devil

John Webster

First performed early in 1612 by The Queen's Men at the Red Bull Theatre in Blackfriars, in London. VITTORIA COROM-BONA, a well-born Venetian Lady and mistress to the Duke of Brachiano, has been tried and condemned as a whore and possible accessory to the murder of her husband, Camillo. She has been sent to the House of Convertites – a place of correction for penitent whores. In this scene, she is visited by the Duke and her brother, Flamineo. The Duke accuses her of receiving love letters and, when she protests her innocence, curses her, calling on the name of his dead Duchess. Furious, VITTORIA hits back, accusing him in return of being responsible for his wife's death and her own ruin.

Act 4, Scene 2

VITTORIA
You did name your Duchess . . . Whose death God revenge
On thee most godless Duke . . .
What have I gain'd by thee but infamy?
Thou hast stain'd the spotless honour of my house,
And frighted thence noble society:
Like those, which sick o'th' palsy, and retain
Ill-scenting foxes 'bout them, are still shunn'd
By those of choicer nostrils. What do you call this house?
Is this your palace? Did not the judge style it
A house of penitent whores? Who sent me to it?
Who hath the honour to advance Vittoria
To this incontinent college? Is't not you?
Is't not your high preferment? Go, go brag
How many ladies you have undone, like me.
Fare you well sir; let me hear no more of you.
I had a limb corrupted to an ulcer,
But I have cut it off: and now I'll go
Weeping to heaven on crutches. For your gifts,
I will return them all; and I do wish
That I could make you full executor
To all my sins. O that I could toss myself
Into a grave as quickly: for all thou art worth
I'll not shed one tear more; – I'll burst first.
[*She throws herself upon a bed*]

The Witch

Thomas Middleton

This Jacobean tragi-comedy was probably written in 1615 or 1616 and performed by The King's Men at Blackfriars, in London. It is set in Ravenna, a token location which could as easily be London, with its satire of life at Court and the King's obsession with witchcraft. The Witch, HECATE, and her sisters are highly comic characters, hovering in the air, baking dead children and, despite their great age, bedding desirable young men and, on occasion, even having their wicked way with Malkin the cat. In this scene HECATE is visited by Sebastian, who begs her to stop the consummation of the marriage between Antonio and Isabella – the girl he still loves and was betrothed to before he went away to war.

Act 1, Scene 2

HECATE
Thy boldness takes me bravely. We're all sworn
To sweat for such a spirit. See, I regard thee,
I rise and bid thee welcome. What's thy wish now? . . .
Is't to confound some enemy on the seas?
It may be done tonight. Stadlin's within;
She raises all your sudden, ruinous storms
That shipwreck barks and tears up growing oaks,
Flies over houses and takes *Anno Domini*
Out of a rich man's chimney – a sweet place for't!
He would be hanged ere he would set his own years there;
They must be chambered in a five-pound picture,
A green silk curtain drawn before the eyes on't,
His rotten diseased years. Or dost thou envy
The fat prosperity of any neighbour?
I'll call forth Hoppo and her incantation
Can straight destroy the young of all his cattle,

Blast vineyards, orchards, meadows or in one night
Transport his dung, hay, corn, by ricks, whole stacks,
Into thine own ground ...
Is it to starve up generation?
To strike a barrenness in man or woman?
Hah? Did you feel me there? I knew your grief.
                            ... Are these the skins
Of serpents? these of snakes? ...
So sure into what house these are conveyed,
Knit with these charmed and retentive knots,
Neither the man begets nor woman breeds;
No, nor performs the least desires of wedlock,
Being then a mutual duty. I could give thee
Chiroconita, adincantida
Archimadon, marmaritin, calicia,
Which I could sort to villainous barren ends –
But this leads the same way. More I could instance:
As the same needles thrust into their pillows
That sows and socks up dead men in their sheets:
A privy gristle of a man that hangs
After sunset – good, excellent! Yet all's there sir.
                        ... We cannot disjoin wedlock;
'Tis of heaven's fastening. Well may we raise jars,
Jealousies, strifes and heart-burning disagreements,
Like a thick scurf o'er life, as did our master
Upon that patient miracle – but the work itself
Our power cannot disjoint ...

                                 [Sebastian exits]
I know he loves me not, nor there's no hope on't;
'Tis for the love of mischief I do this –
And that we're sworn to, the first oath we take.

takes pleases
bravely a great deal
sworn in compact with the devil
barks boats
Anno Domini the year that the house was built, marked on a stone tablet and placed in the chimney
sweet meant ironically, as a chimney smells of soot
years his age
chambered ... on't They must be recorded in a portrait costing five pounds (which noted the sitter's age)

with a green silk curtain drawn over it.
I knew ... grief typical charlatan's trick, claiming prescience after several wrong guesses
chiroconita ... calicia all poisons
sort arrange
privy gristle i.e. penis
jars discords
our master the devil
that patient miracle Job, whose suffering was a test of faith and of love of God
the work the marriage

121

The Witch

Thomas Middleton

This Jacobean tragi-comedy was probably written in 1615 or 1616 and performed by The King's Men at Blackfriars, in London. It is set in Ravenna, a token location which could easily be London, with its satire of life at Court and the King's obsession with witchcraft. FRANCISCA, a young and innocent girl, has been seduced by Aberzanes, a gentleman described as neither honest, wise nor valiant. It is the day after her brother Antonio's wedding and she has discovered that she is pregnant. She is terrified that her brother will find out and hopes that Aberzanes will find some way of saving her from disgrace.

Act 2, Scene 1

FRANCISCA
I have the hardest fortune, I think of a hundred gentlewomen.
Some can make merry with a friend seven year
And nothing seen – as perfect a maid still,
To the world's knowledge, as she came from rocking.
But 'twas my luck, at the first hour, forsooth,
To prove too fruitful. Sure I'm near my time.
I'm yet but a young scholar, I may fail
In my account – but certainly I do not.

These bastards come upon poor venturing gentlewomen ten to one
faster than your legitimate children. If I had been married, I'll be
hanged if I had been with child so soon now. When they are once
husbands, they'll be whipped ere they take such pains as a friend
will do: to come by water to the backdoor at midnight: there stay
perhaps an hour in all weathers with a pair of reeking watermen
laden with bottles of wine, chewets and currant custards. I may curse
those egg-pies – they are meat that help forward too fast.
This hath been usual with me night by night –

Honesty forgive me – when my brother has been
Dreaming of no such junkets; yet he hath fared
The better for my sake, though he little think
For what – nor must he ever. My friend promised me
To provide safely for me and devise
A means to save my credit here i'th'house.
My brother sure would kill me if he knew't,
And powder up my friend and all his kindred
For an East Indian voyage.

friend lover
rocking in the cradle
venturing gambling or investing sexually
chewets minced meat or fish pies
egg-pies Eggs were regarded as aphrodisiacs.
junkets feastings, merrymakings
powder up preserve meat by salting

123

A Woman Killed with Kindness

Thomas Heywood

First performed in London in 1604 and set in Yorkshire. It is the story of ANNE FRANKFORD, the 'perfect wife' of John Frankford, her infidelity with Wendoll, her husband's trusted friend, and the extraordinary punishment meted out to her by her husband of 'extreme kindness' which leads to her eventual death. In this scene Frankford has returned home to find ANNE and Wendoll lying in each other's arms. He runs after Wendoll with drawn sword, but is prevented from killing him by the Maid who 'stays his hand' as ANNE enters in her night attire. As she speaks she expects Frankford to be angry with her, but instead he is gentle almost seeming to blame himself.

Scene 13

ANNE
O by what word, what title, or what name
Shall I entreat your pardon? Pardon! O
I am as far from hoping such sweet grace
As Lucifer from heaven. To call you husband!
O me most wretched, I have lost that name;
I am no more your wife . . .
I would I had no tongue, no ears, no eyes,
No apprehension, no capacity.
When do you spurn me like a dog? When tread me
Under your feet? When drag me by the hair?
Though I deserve a thousand thousandfold
More than you can inflict, yet, once my husband,
For womanhood – to which I am shame
Though once an ornament – even for His sake
That hath redeemed our souls, mark not my face
Nor hack me with your sword, but let me go
Perfect and undeformed to my tomb.
I am not worthy that I should prevail
In the least suit, no, not to speak to you.
Nor look on you, nor to be in your presence.
Yet, as an abject, this one suit I crave;
This granted, I am ready for my grave.

A Woman of No Importance

Oscar Wilde

This society comedy or comedy of manners was first produced in 1893 at the Haymarket Theatre, London, and set mainly at the country home of the influential Lady Hunstanton. HESTER WORSLEY, a young, very pretty but forthright American, who entertained Lady Hunstanton's son when he visited Boston recently, has been invited down to Hunstanton Chase for the weekend. In this scene, Lady Hunstanton, concerned lest HESTER may have overheard and be shocked by the drawing-room conversation of English society ladies, and in particular the notorious Mrs Allonby, tells her young guest not to believe everything she hears. HESTER retorts that 'she couldn't believe that any women could really hold such views of life' and when the ladies' remarks are directed to her personally, shows that she is more than a match for any of them.

Act 2

HESTER

The English aristocracy supply us with our curiosities, Lady Caroline. They are sent over to us every summer, regularly, in the steamers, and propose to us the day after they land. As for ruins, we are trying to build up something that will last longer than brick or stone.

[Gets up to take her fan from table] . . .

[Standing by table]

We are trying to build up life, Lady Hunstanton, on a better, truer, purer basis than life rests on here. This sounds strange to you all, no doubt. How could it sound other than strange? You rich people in England, you don't know how you are living. How could you know? You shut out from your society the gentle and the good. You laugh at the simple and the pure. Living, as you all do, on others and by them, you sneer at self-sacrifice, and if you throw bread to the poor, it is merely to keep them quiet for a season. With all your pomp and wealth and art you don't know how to live – you don't even know that. You love the beauty that you can see and touch and handle, the beauty that you can destroy, and do destroy, but of the unseen beauty of life, of the unseen beauty of a higher life, you know nothing. You have lost life's secret. Oh, your English society seems to me shallow, selfish, foolish. It has blinded its eyes, and stopped its ears. It lies like a leper in purple. It sits like a dead thing smeared with gold. It is all wrong, all wrong . . . Lord Henry Weston! I remember him, Lady Hunstanton. A man with a hideous smile and a hideous past. He is asked everywhere. No dinner-party is complete without him. What of those whose ruin is due to him? They are outcasts. They are nameless. If you met them in the street you would turn your head away. I don't complain of their punishment. Let all women who have sinned be punished . . . It is right that they should be punished, but don't let them be the only ones to suffer. If a man and woman have sinned, let them both go forth into the desert to love or loathe each other there. Let them both be branded. Set a mark, if you wish, on each, but don't punish the one and let the other go free. Don't have one law for men and another for women. You are unjust to women in England. And till you count what is a shame in a woman to be an infamy in a man, you will always be unjust, and Right, that pillar of fire, and Wrong, that pillar of cloud, will be made dim to your eyes, or be not seen at all, or if seen, not regarded.

Women Beware Women

Thomas Middleton

There is no record of this Jacobean revenge tragedy until well after Middleton's death, but it was most likely written in 1621 and performed with great success. A play of love, lust, incest and revenge, it exposes the position of women in a world where, at best, they are simply the property of men whatever their social status may be. LIVIA, a rich, older but still attractive woman, who has already had two husbands, is attracted to Leantio, a young and not very successful commercial agent. Leantio is heartbroken because his wife, Bianca, has left him and is now the official mistress of the Duke of Florence. In this scene, after a banquet attended by the Duke with Bianca on his arm, Leantio pours out his grief, hardly aware of LIVIA's presence. She offers herself to him, promising to give him whatever he desires, but he can think of nothing but Bianca.

Act 3, Scene 2

LIVIA

                           Then first, sir,
To make away all your good thoughts at once of her,
Know most assuredly she is a strumpet . . .
You missed your fortunes when you met with her, sir.
Young gentlemen that only love for beauty,
They love not wisely; such a marriage rather
Proves the destruction of affection –
It brings on want, and want's the key of whoredom.
I think y'had small means with her . . .
Alas, poor gentleman, what meant'st thou, sir,
Quite to undo thyself with thine own kind heart?
Thou art too good and pitiful to woman.

Marry, sir, thank thy stars for this blest fortune
That rids the summer of thy youth so well
From many beggars that had lain a-sunning
In thy beams only else, till thou hadst wasted
The whole days of thy life in heat and labour.
What would you say now to a creature found
As pitiful to you, and as it were
Ev'n sent on purpose from the whole sex general,
To requite all that kindness you have shown to't?
                    . . . Nay, a gentlewoman, and one able
To reward good things, ay, and bears a conscience to't.
Could'st thou love such a one, that – blow all fortunes –
Would never see thee want?
Nay more, maintain thee to thine enemy's envy?
And shalt not spend a care for't, stir a thought,
Nor break a sleep, unless love's music waked thee;
No storm of fortune should. Look upon me,
And know that woman.
[LEANTIO. . . Oh my life's wealth, Bianca!]
Still with her name? Will nothing wear it out?
That deep sigh went but for a strumpet, sir. . . .
[Aside] He's vexed in mind; I came too soon to him;
Where's my discretion now, my skill, my judgement?
I'm cunning in all arts but my own love.
'Tis as unseasonable to tempt him now
So soon, as a widow to be courted
Following her husband's corse, or to make bargain
By the grave-side, and take a young man there:
Her strange departure stands like a hearse yet
Before his eyes, which time will take down shortly.

small means i.e. she had no real dowry
sex general all women
blow all fortunes i.e. come what may
And shalt and you shall
strange like a stranger; not yet familiar
hearse a wooden structure erected over a coffin for a certain period of time

Women Beware Women

Thomas Middleton

There is no record of this Jacobean revenge tragedy until well after Middleton's death, but it was most likely written in 1621 and performed with great success. A play of love, lust, incest and revenge, it exposes the position of women in a world where, at best, they are simply the property of men whatever their social status may be. BIANCA CAPELLO, a young Venetian heiress, has eloped with Leantio, a not very successful commercial agent, who takes her home to live with him and his elderly mother. She is seen by the Duke of Florence, who falls in love with her, seduces her and makes her his mistress. His brother, the Cardinal, strongly disapproves of the relationship and warns of eternal damnation. In this scene, the Duke, having arranged for the murder of Leantio, is about to marry BIANCA. They are interrupted by the Cardinal demanding that the ceremony cease. It will 'pull Heaven's thunder down upon Florence.' BIANCA defies him in this speech and the Duke orders the service to continue.

Act 4, Scene 3

BIANCA

Sir, I have read you over all this while
In silence, and I find great knowledge in you,
And severe learning; yet 'mongst all your virtues
I see not charity written, which some call
The first-born of religion, and I wonder
I cannot see't in yours. Believe it, sir,
There is no virtue can be sooner missed
Or later welcomed; it begins the rest,
And sets 'em all in order. Heaven and angels
Take great delight in a converted sinner;
Why should you, then, a servant and professor,
Differ so much from them? If ev'ry woman
That commits evil should be therefore kept
Back in desires of goodness, how should virtue
Be known and honoured? From a man that's blind
To take a burning taper, 'tis no wrong,
He never misses it; but to take light
From one that sees, that's injury and spite.
Pray, whether is religion better served,
When lives that are licentious are made honest,
Than when they still run through a sinful blood?
'Tis nothing virtue's temples to deface;
But build the ruins, there's a work of grace.

read you over closely observed you
professor one who professes knowledge (here, one who professes to be a Christian)
Than or
blood desire

Index of playwrights

Anon
  Arden of Faversham
  The Revenger's Tragedy
Francis Beaumont
  The Knight of the Burning Pestle
Aphra Behn
  The Rover
George Chapman
  Bussy D'Ambois
William Congreve
  The Double-Dealer
  Love for Love
  The Way of the World
Thomas Dekker
  The Shoemaker's Holiday
John Dryden
  All for Love
George Farquhar
  The Beaux' Stratagem
John Ford
  The Broken Heart
  'Tis Pity She's a Whore
Oliver Goldsmith
  She Stoops to Conquer
Thomas Heywood
  A Woman Killed with Kindness
Ben Jonson
  The Alchemist
  Bartholmew Fair
  Epicoene *or* The Silent Woman
Ben Jonson, George Chapman &
John Marston
  Eastward Ho!

Thomas Kyd
  The Spanish Tragedy
Christopher Marlowe
  Edward the Second
John Marston
  The Malcontent
Thomas Middleton
  The Witch
  Women Beware Women
Thomas Middleton & William
Rowley
  The Changeling
  A Fair Quarrel
Richard Brinsley Sheridan
  The Critic
  The Rivals
  The School for Scandal
Cyril Tourneur
  The Atheist's Tragedy
John Vanbrugh
  The Provoked Wife
  The Relapse
John Webster
  The Duchess of Malfi
  The White Devil
Oscar Wilde
  An Ideal Husband
  The Importance of Being Earnest
  Lady Windermere's Fan
  A Woman of No Importance
William Wycherley
  The Country Wife
  The Plain Dealer

ORDER FORM

The New Mermaid play texts can be ordered from your local bookseller or direct from our warehouse. In the USA and Canada customers can order the play texts through W.W. Norton & Company, 500 Fifth Avenue, New York NY 10110.

The Alchemist Ben Jonson £4.99
All for Love John Dryden £4.99
Arden of Faversham Anon £4.99
The Atheist's Tragedy Cyril Tourneur £4.99
Bartholmew Fair Ben Jonson £5.99
The Beaux' Stratagem George Farquhar £4.99
The Broken Heart John Ford £5.99
Bussy D'Ambois George Chapman £4.99
The Changeling Thomas Middleton & William Rowley £4.99
The Country Wife William Wycherley £4.99
The Critic Richard Brinsley Sheridan £4.99
The Double-Dealer William Congreve £4.99
The Duchess of Malfi John Webster £4.99
Eastward Ho! Ben Jonson, George Chapman & John Marston £5.99
Edward the Second Christopher Marlowe £4.99
Epicoene or *the Silent Woman* Ben Jonson £5.99
A Fair Quarrel Thomas Middleton & William Rowley £4.99
An Ideal Husband Oscar Wilde £5.99
The Importance of Being Earnest Oscar Wilde £4.99
The Knight of the Burning Pestle Francis Beaumont £4.99
Lady Windermere's Fan Oscar Wilde £4.99
Love for Love William Congreve £4.99
The Malcontent John Marston £4.99
The Plain Dealer William Wycherley £4.99
The Provoked Wife John Vanbrugh £5.99
The Relapse John Vanbrugh £5.99
The Revenger's Tragedy Anon £4.99
The Rivals Richard Brinsley Sheridan £4.99
The Rover Aphra Behn £5.99
The School for Scandal Richard Brinsley Sheridan £4.99
She Stoops to Conquer Oliver Goldsmith £4.99

The Shoemaker's Holiday Thomas Dekker £4.99
The Spanish Tragedy Thomas Kyd £4.99
'Tis Pity She's a Whore John Ford £4.99
Volpone Ben Jonson £4.99
The Way of the World William Congreve £4.99
The White Devil John Webster £5.99
The Witch Thomas Middleton £5.99
A Woman Killed with Kindness Thomas Heywood £4.99
A Woman of No Importance Oscar Wilde £5.99
Women Beware Women Thomas Middleton £5.99

Tick the title(s) you want and fill in the form below.
Prices and availability subject to change without notice

Please return to **A & C Black (Publishers) Limited, PO Box 19, Huntingdon, Cambs PE19 3SF tel (01480) 212666 fax (01480) 405014**

Send a cheque or postal order for the value of the book(s), adding (for postage and packing at the printed paper rate) 15% UK and Eire; 20% overseas.
Airmail rates available on application

Or please debit this amount from my Access/Visa Card (delete as appropriate)

Card number

Amount _____   Expiry date

Signed _____

Name (please print)_____

Address_____

_____   Postcode _____